Ukrainians
in the *Waffen-SS*

Ukrainians in the *Waffen-SS*

The *14. Waffen-Grenadier-Division der SS (ukrainische Nr. 1)*

Rolf Michaelis

Schiffer Military History
Atglen, PA

Book Translation by David Johnston

Book Design by Stephanie Daugherty.

Copyright © 2009 by Schiffer Publishing.
Library of Congress Control Number: 2009929044

Printed in China.
ISBN: 978-0-7643-3349-1
This book was originally published in German under the title
Ukrainer in der Waffen-SS
Die 14. Waffen-Grenadier-Division der SS (ukrainische Nr.1)

We are interested in hearing from authors with book ideas on related topics.

Published by Schiffer Publishing Ltd.
4880 Lower Valley Road
Atglen, PA 19310
Phone: (610) 593-1777
FAX: (610) 593-2002
E-mail: Info@schifferbooks.com.
Visit our web site at: www.schifferbooks.com
Please write for a free catalog.
This book may be purchased from the publisher.
Please include $5.00 postage.
Try your bookstore first.

In Europe, Schiffer books are distributed by:
Bushwood Books
6 Marksbury Avenue
Kew Gardens
Surrey TW9 4JF, England
Phone: 44 (0) 20 8392-8585
FAX: 44 (0) 20 8392-9876
E-mail: Info@bushwoodbooks.co.uk.
Visit our website at: www.bushwoodbooks.co.uk

Table of Contents

Foreword

In 1939/40 the armed formations of the *Schutzstaffel*[1] were combined under the title *Waffen-SS*. Intended by Himmler to be an elite National-Socialist fighting organization, its strength grew from about 120,000 members in early 1940 to approximately 600,000 men in 1945. During the Second World War more than a million men from all over Europe served more or less voluntarily in the ranks of the *Waffen-SS*. Among them were about 40,000 Ukrainians.

The purpose of this book is to document them and the history of the *14. Waffen-Grenadier-Division der SS (ukrainische Nr. 1)*. How did this foreign division, which was in fact contrary to Hitler's *Ostpolitik*, come to be formed? What equipment, scope, and training did it have and where was it committed? What motivated the Ukrainians to serve in this division and how good was its morale? Did the unit achieve military success and what was its fate at the end of the war?

In writing this book I was able to call upon the memories of German and Ukrainian soldiers to supplement the documents in foreign and German archives. In the hope that this publication will shed some light on an unknown part of German-European military history, I thank those who supported me in writing this book.

Berlin, March 2000
Rolf Michaelis

Formation of the Division

After the defeat before Moscow in 1941 it became clear to the German army command that the campaign in the east could not be won in a *Blitzkrieg*. At that time Hitler still held to the view he had expressed in the summer of 1941:

"No one but the Germans must ever be allowed to bear arms! This is of particular importance; even if it appears easier at first to employ some foreign subject people to assist our armies, it is wrong! One day it will definitely and unavoidably turn against us. Only the Germans must bear arms, not the Slavs, not the Czechs, not the Cossacks or Ukrainians."

Nevertheless, various German civilian and military offices were already making plans to use foreign volunteers to help in the struggle.

But it was not until the Allied successes at Stalingrad and Tunis in early 1943, when hundreds of thousands of German and Allied troops were captured, that opportunism led Hitler to revise his previous position. He modified his *Ostpolitik*, and in February 1943 declared that nations threatened by the Soviet Union should join the defensive front against bolshevism. He had finally realized that the German armed services were incapable of holding the occupied territories and simultaneously bringing the war to a victorious conclusion.

The governor of the District of Galicia,[1] Dr. Wächter,[2] was aware of the military situation and, seeing the unexploited potential of men capable of military service in his area of administration, on 4 March 1943 he proposed to the *Reichsführer-SS* that a division be formed from West-Ukrainian volunteers.

Himmler took up the idea on 28 March 1943 with the approval of Hitler. The latter saw the possibility of exploiting the potential of the old Imperial Austrian territory of Galicia, while Himmler was interested in a new source of recruits for his *Waffen-SS*. Already on 6 April 1943 *SS-Gruppenführer* Berger[3] informed the *Reichsführer-SS* that a special recruiting committee had been formed. Two days later Professor Kubiyovich, head of the largely symbolic Ukrainian Central Committee, offered his support in establishing a Ukrainian division.

As the *Waffen-SS* was chronically short of officers and NCOs, a situation aggravated by heavy casualties and the formation and reformation of many units, *SS-Gruppenführer* Berger initially declared that the *Waffen-SS* was not in a position to provide the necessary core personnel for the establishment of a new division. Instead, he proposed that the volunteers be incorporated into a formation of the *Ordnungspolizei* (Order Police)—similar to the first Police Division.[4]

At a meeting in April 1943, however, Dr. Wächter vehemently opposed designating the formation of a police unit; the military aspect was to be stressed by the title "Volunteer Division Galicia." Himmler ultimately fell in line and ordered that the formation of the division would be exclusively a matter for the *Waffen-SS*. The shortfall of core personnel would be made good by the *Ordnungspolizei*,

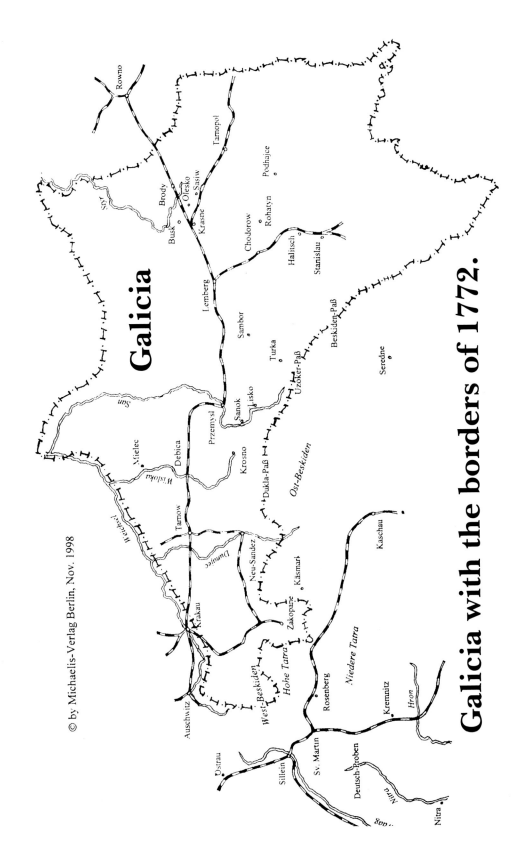

Galicia

Galicia with the borders of 1772.

© by Michaelis-Verlag Berlin, Nov. 1998

The District of Galicia as part of the General Government.

Ostsee

Pommern

Tilsit

Kauen

Wilna

Königsberg Insterburg

Reichskommissariat
Ostland

Danzig Elbing Rastenburg

Marienburg

Ostpreußen

Lida

Grodno

Westpreußen

Bz. Bialystok

Bromberg Thorn

Bialystok

Posen

Wartheland

Warschau Siedlce

Distrikt Warschau

Brest-Litowsk

Lissa Kalisch Litzmannstadt

Petrikau Radom

Lublin

Kowel

Nieder-

Breslau

Kielce

Distrikt Lublin

Reichskommissariat
Ukraine

Schlesien Distrikt Radom

Zamosc

Brieg Tschenstochau Sokal

Oppeln Generalgouvernement

Brody

Kattowitz Reichshof Lemberg

Krakau Tarnopol

Oberschlesien

Ost-
Sudeten-
land Troppau Distrikt Krakau Distrikt Galizien

Stanislau

Olmütz Sillein Kolomyja

Protektorat
Böhmen/

Brünn Slowakei Ungvar Rumänien

Mähren Kaschau

Miskolc

Ungarn

Pressburg

Debrecen

© by Michaelis-Verlag Berlin, Nov. 1998

The 11th Company of the SS Special Purpose Training Battalion of the SS Volunteer Rifle Division Galicia.

however. About this, *SS-Oberstgruppenführer* Daluege,[5] head of the *Ordnungspolizei*, noted on 14 April 1943:

> "*A frontline division is being established for the Waffen-SS and by the Waffen-SS, which will consist of Greek-Catholic Ukrainians and will probably be called the Galician Division; for these Ukrainians come from Galicia. The remaining Ukrainians in the General-Government, from the Lublin area, are Greek-Orthodox.[6] They are being made available to us for the establishment of police regiments, which means with only a few German officers...*"

Four days later the Ukrainian defense committee met for the first time. On 28 April 1943, even before the establishment formation order was issued by the SS-FHA, General Governor Dr. Frank and District Governor Dr. Wächter officially informed the Galician population that the division was being formed. The next day the Cracow Times reported the "*Formation of an SS Rifle Division Galicia for the Ukrainian youth:*"[7]

> "*Active participation by the Galician-Ukrainian population in the European freedom struggle against the Soviet Union in its own unit made possible—formation of a Galician Defense Committee*
>
> *After the Führer authorized the formation of a Galician-Ukrainian military unit in response to the oft-expressed wish of the Galician-Ukrainian population and in recognition of its positive political attitude and cooperation, yesterday in the Statthalter Palace in Lvov the governor of the District of Galicia, SS-Brigadeführer Wächter, announced the formation of the SS Rifle Division Galicia before representatives of the state, armed services, party, representatives of the Ukrainian people and senior Ukrainian religious officials.*
>
> *The SS Rifle Division Galicia will be made up of young Galician-Ukrainian volunteers, who will assume the responsibility of continuing an old tradition of military service, which once allied their forefathers in the Austrian Army with the Germans. The soldiers of the SS Rifle Division Galicia have the same rights and obligations as the soldiers of the Wehrmacht, which of course includes caring for their families. The members of the unit will wear a national emblem consisting of three golden crowns from the Theresian period and the heraldic lion, symbol of the oldest Ukrainian mastery of Galician soil by Prince Halitch, against a blue field. The SS Rifle Division Galicia is a unit of the Waffen-SS and therefore a frontline unit, which as such represents the desire of the Ukrainian people to go beyond their previous participation in the building of a new Europe as farmers, administrators and workers in the Reich, and take up arms to prove themselves in the front lines against bolshevism. After necessary retraining, the division's leadership corps will consist of Ukrainian officers and NCOs who can prove previous military training in the former Austrian Army or the Polish Army. The language of command will be German, the language of orders Ukrainian. [...]*"

80,000 volunteers reported within four weeks.[8] 50,000 of these were accepted on an interim basis by 3 June 1944. Of 15,000 mustered only about 15% were usable, however.[9] It was calculated that there would be a total of about 25,000 Ukrainians fit for active service. As a rule the enlisted men were between 17 and 30 years old, and most had an agricultural background. Some of the older men had

Collar Patches

woven version   embroidered version

Enlisted men and non-commissioned officers

embroidered version   embroidered version for officers of the 1st Division of the Ukrainian National Army

served in the Imperial Army or in the Polish and Ukrainian Armies.[10] With respect to so-called "SS suitability," the only requirement for the volunteers was a height of at least 165 cm.[11]

Although recruiting was already under way, it was not until three months later, on 30 July 1943, that the SS-FHA[12] announced that Hitler had ordered the formation of an **SS Volunteer Division Galicia**.[13]

The Galician *SS-Ausbildungs-Bataillon z.b.V.* (SS Special Purpose Training Battalion), which was already stationed at the SS training camp at Heidelager (Debica), was to form the core of the division. Also to be established were:

> SS Volunteer Regiment 1 (3 battalions)
> SS Volunteer Regiment 2 (3 battalions)
> SS Volunteer Regiment 3 (3 battalions)
> SS Flak Battalion
> SS Volunteer Artillery Regiment (4 battalions)
> SS Signals Battalion
> SS Pioneer Battalion
> SS Reconnaissance Battalion
> SS Anti-Tank Battalion
> SS Economic Battalion
> SS Medical Battalion
> SS Veterinary Company

The oath sworn by the volunteers read as follows:

"I swear before God this sacred oath, that, in the struggle against bolshevism, I will render unconditional loyalty to Adolf Hitler, supreme commander of the German armed services, and as a brave soldier will be ready to lay down my life at any time for this oath."[14]

Initially responsible for the establishment of the division, whose language of command was Ukrainian but whose language of orders was German, was *SS-Brigadeführer* Schimana.[15] To outwardly differentiate them from the German and so-called Germanic SS members, instead of *Sig-Runen* on the right collar patch the Ukrainians were to wear plain black patches with an embroidered Galician lion.[16] As well, a blue sleeve badge was sewn onto the left upper sleeve, onto which the heraldic lion with three crowns was woven in gold-yellow thread.

Volunteers arrived in Debica daily. On 22 September 1943 the SS-FHA[17] announced the reorganization of the formation, which was henceforth titled the *14. Galizische SS-Freiwilligen-Infanterie-Division* (14th Galician SS Volunteer Infantry Division). The division's composition was as follows:

> Division Headquarters[18]
> SS Volunteer Grenadier Regiment 29 (just 2 battalions)
> SS Volunteer Grenadier Regiment 30 (ditto)
> SS Volunteer Grenadier Regiment 31 (ditto)
> SS Fusilier Battalion 14
> SS Volunteer Artillery Regiment 14 (4 battalions)

**Swearing-in of an SS volunteer regiment
at the Heidelager training camp in the summer of 1943.**

**The oath was read out by the German regimental commander
and translated by an interpreter.**

The regiment in square formation.

Officers inspect the troops.

Front left: *SS-Brigadeführer* **Dr. Wächter**
in the center: *SS-Brigadeführer* **Voß**
front right: *SS-Obersturmbannführer* **Herms**

The regiment marches off after the swearing-in.

Return to barracks.

**26 August 1943: a group of Ukrainian entertainers
visits the volunteers at the SS training camp in Heidelager.**

The entertainers wearing traditional Galician garb.

Entertainers and troops enjoy some happy moments after the show.

SS Field Replacement Battalion 14
SS Pioneer Battalion 14
SS Anti-Tank Battalion 14
SS Signals Battalion 14
SS Economic Battalion 14
SS Medical Battalion 14
SS Veterinary Battalion 14

SS-Brigadeführer Dr. Wächter and *SS-Brigadeführer* Voß,[19] commander of the Debica SS training camp, both took part in one of the first swearing-in ceremonies in the summer of 1943. One month later Himmler relieved *SS-Brigadeführer* Schimana of command of the formation headquarters of the *14. Galizische SS-Freiwilligen-Infanterie-Division* and handed command over to *SS-Oberführer* Freitag.[20] In autumn 1943 60 officers and 200 NCOs were sent to the appropriate schools for additional training in order to later fill these positions within the division.

An appeal to the Ukrainian population in Galicia in December 1943 resulted in the *14. Galizische SS-Freiwilligen-Infanterie-Division* and the Galician SS volunteer regiments of the Order Police receiving numerous donations. The following is an excerpt from a report by the Senior SS and Police Commander East:

"Subsequent to my telex of 16/12/43, I am informing you that, according to another report by the governor of the District of Galicia, SS-Brigadeführer Wächter, the population in his area have made donations to members of the Galician SS volunteer units totaling 400,000 Zl. [zloty]. From these donations the Military Board of Galicia has had produced 20,000 Christmas packages each containing 2 kg of goods.

As an additional Christmas gift to the 14. Galizische SS-Freiwilligen-Infanterie-Division the Military Board of Galicia has given its commander 100,000 RM plus 25,000 RM in cash to each of the Galician SS volunteer regiments. For preparation of Kutya, the traditional Christmas dish consisting of steamed wheat, poppy seeds and honey, the Military Board of Galicia has sent the SS volunteer units 20 quintals of wheat, 4 quintals of poppy seeds and 4 quintals of honey. Needy family members of the Galician SS volunteers received Christmas packages of clothing and commodities with a total value of 400,000 Zl. 100,000 Zl. was spent on Galician entertainers sent to put on Christmas shows for the SS volunteer units. Therefore the Military Board of Galicia has spent a total of 1,300,000 Zl. on the Galician volunteer units for the 1943 Christmas holiday from the donations made by the population.

I ask that you bring this exemplary charitable effort, which demonstrates a considerable willingness by the Galician population to make sacrifices for the benefit of their SS volunteers, to the attention of the Reichsführer-SS..."

A report by the SS-FHA dated 31 December 1943 gave the strength of the SS Volunteer Division Galicia as:

Officers	NCOs	Enlisted Men	Total	
256	449	11,929	12,634	actual strength
2%	3.5%	94.5%	100%	
480	2,587	11,682	14,749	authorized strength
3.3%	17.5%	79.2%	100%	

The unit was thus short approximately 2,200 officers and NCOs, a condition that made it impossible for the division to undertake any combat operations.[21] Nevertheless, at the beginning of February 1944 the Senior Police and SS Commander East, *SS-Obergruppenführer und General der Polizei* Wilhelm Koppe,[22] ordered the division to form a regiment-strength battle group for anti-partisan operations. On 16 February 1944, under the command of *SS-Obersturmbannführer* Beyersdorff, the SS battle group, consisting of

- one motorized grenadier battalion (*SS-Sturmbannführer* Bristot)
- a heavy battalion (*SS-Sturmbannführer* Paliyenko),

was transported on three trains into the Lublin district. Its mission was to engage approximately 2,000 national Polish partisans believed to be in the wooded areas near Zamosc. On 20 March 1944, having met with no success, SS Battle Group Beyersdorff was sent back to the division.

The division had meanwhile been bolstered through the addition of Galician SS Volunteer Regiments 6 and 7[23] and moved from Debica to Neuhammer, as the former camp had proved unsuitable for the establishment of the division. It was not an secure area; consequently, there were always civilians on the grounds, or soldiers left without permission.

The addition of the Ukrainians from the Order Police made possible the formation of SS Field Replacement Battalion 14 (strength: 800 men) at the Wandern training camp near Frankfurt/Oder in Aril 1944, as well as SS Grenadier Replacement Training Regiment 14. Myron Pryjma was just 15 years old when he volunteered, and in April 1944 he was assigned toss Field Replacement Battalion 14:

"I was born in Lvov in March 1929, the son of Pastor Myron Pryjma. My father was editor of Neta (Goal), the parish newsletter, and gathered information about the famine in the years 1932/33. He published a book about this tragedy under the initials M.P. Not using his full name with this work later saved his life. He was arrested by the Bolsheviks on 25 November 1940 and banished to Siberia for 15 years.

When the German troops came to Lvov, my mother, grandmother and I—like thousands of others—looked for him in the many prisons. We saw hundreds of bodies but didn't find him. It wasn't until later that we learned that he had been sent to Siberia before the war.

I attended the people's school and then a secondary school, which was closed when the Russians approached Galicia in March 1944. I then joined the Galicia Division as a volunteer. Just to be accepted I had to tell them I was two years older. Not long afterwards, in the first days of April 1944, I arrived at the division's field replacement battalion at the Neuhammer training camp..."

Anton Hrycszyn described what motivated him to join the Galician Division:

"I was born in Krive (Galicia) in 1921. In 1941 I answered the appeal to work in Germany. I went to BMW in Munich, but I was sent home again as I allegedly had tuberculosis. Then in 1942 I was supposed to be taken into the labor service. I didn't like that much and so I went to Berezhany, where I was finally arrested and locked up for a few

The sleeve badge of the 14th Galician SS Volunteer Division (enlarged).

SS-Oberführer **Freitag administers the oath to Ukrainian volunteers, autumn 1943.**

SS-Oberführer **Freitag with German core personnel.**

Taking the oath at the Heidelager SS training camp.

days. During that time I and several other prisoners were forced to dig a mass grave in the local cemetery and witnessed the shooting of several hundred Jews.

After this massacre I was sent to a German punishment camp near Skole in the Carpathians. I subsequently escaped with the assistance of the UPA. I initially returned to Krive but then I went to Ternopol with the labor service. In 1944 we Ukrainian members of the labor service in the General Government were brought to Berezhany and there were given the choice of either joining the Todt Organization in Germany or going to the 14th SS Division.

I chose to join the division, as I feared that I might be imprisoned again for escaping from the punishment camp. In May 1944 I became a member of the Galician Division and was sent to Kirchbaum for training."

On 16 May 1944, one year after formation began, Himmler and Dr. Wächter paid a visit to the division. The unit gave mock combat demonstrations and there was a marchpast by various units. Himmler was extremely satisfied by the level of training and declared that the unit could expect to see action soon with Army Group North Ukraine, as it was expected that the Red Army was going to advance against the army group from the Ternopol—Kovel area. The later *SS-Obersturmführer* Bernhard Dornbusch remembered:

"I was born in Lausitz on 11 January 1918 and on 30 November 1939 I joined II Battalion/SS Artillery Replacement Battalion in Berlin-Lichterfelde. I participated in the western campaign as a member of the Leibstandarte. On 1 September 1940 I went to the SS Medical Academy in Graz to study. I subsequently attended the SS officer school in Bad Tölz and in March 1944 was assigned to the 14th Galician SS Volunteer Infantry Division. My first assignment there was as adjutant of II Battalion/ SS Volunteer Grenadier Regiment 29.

I remember Himmler's visit to the Neuhammer training camp very well. After a mock combat, while parading before Himmler I strove to maintain the proper distance from my battalion commander while 'on horseback.' I subsequently drove to the registry office in Lipschau-Dohms to get married and then returned in time to hear Himmler's speech in the mess at Neuhammer. It was a very long evening and we officers were assembled to hear Himmler. His speech was translated into Ukrainian—but I can no longer remember its contents. He came with just a small entourage and the next day left the training camp. As I took advantage of the marriage leave that was due me, I was relieved as adjutant and after my return I was transferred to the field replacement battalion's heavy company."

The division commander addresses his men, Christmas 1943.

Action at Brody

In mid-June 1944 a discussion took place between *Generalfeldmarschall* Model,[24] commander-in-chief of Army Group North Ukraine, and *SS-Brigadeführer* Freitag concerning the employment of the division, which on 27 June 1944 was renamed the *14. Waffen-Grenadier-Division der SS (galizische Nr. 1)*. At that time its strength was:

Officers	NCOs	Enlisted Men	Total
346	1,131	13,822	15,299 actual
2.3%	7.4%	90.3%	100%
480	2,587	11,682	14,749 authorized
3.3%	17.5%	79.2%	100%

Although the division had made some progress in addressing the shortfall in officers and NCOs in the previous year, these positions remained very weakly manned. As a result, operational employment of the division was almost out of the question.

On 25 June 1944 an advance detachment left the Neuhammer training camp to prepare quarters in the area of operations. Three days later the transfer of the division into the 4th Panzer Army's area began. Attached to the XIII Army Corps[25] west of Brody (96 km east of Lvov), it occupied the second line, approximately 12 km behind the main line of resistance, from Stanislawczyk to north of Maidan. *Waffen-Grenadier-Regiment der SS 31* was on the left wing, *Waffen-Grenadier-Regiment der SS 30* in the center, and *Waffen-Grenadier-Regiment der SS 29* on the division's right wing. Elements of the *14. Waffen-Grenadier-Division der SS* saw action against Soviet partisans in the Olesko—Padhorce—Konty area.[26]

In front of this line, approximately 36 km long, units of the XIII Army Corps manned the front around Brody: the 454th Security Division, the 349th and 361st Infantry Divisions, and *Korps-Abteilung C* (Corps Detachment C). At the beginning of July 1944 the 1st Panzer Army's boundary was pushed north; consequently, the XIII Army Corps came under its command.

On Thursday, 13 July 1944, following a heavy artillery bombardment and massive air attacks, the 1st Ukrainian Front (Marshall Konev) attacked Army Group North Ukraine with 80 rifle divisions and ten tank and mechanized brigades as part of the Soviet summer offensive. Two days later Soviet troops attacked the 454th Security Division at the boundary between the XIII and XXXXII Army Corps in the Boldury area. In the south the enemy broke into the Podkamien—Ternopol line held by the 349th Infantry Division at the boundary with the neighboring XXXXVIII Panzer Corps. In a few hours the Red Army had gained an area about 50 km wide and 15 km deep.

As a result of this development, *SS-Brigadeführer* Freitag received orders to pull his division out of the second line and ready it for a counterattack between Maidan and Sasov. The resulting first action by *Waffen-Grenadier-Regiment der SS 30* ended

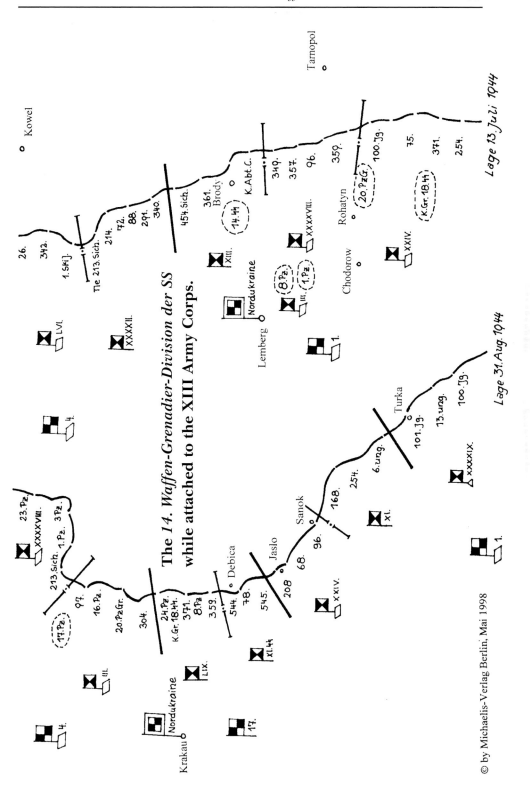

The 14. Waffen-Grenadier-Division der SS
while attached to the XIII Army Corps.

Lage 13. Juli 1944

Lage 31. Aug. 1944

© by Michaelis-Verlag Berlin, Mai 1998

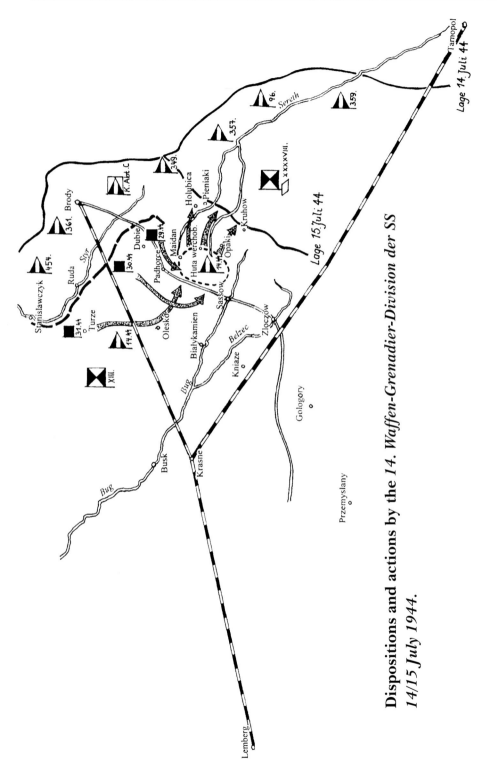

Dispositions and actions by the 14. Waffen-Grenadier-Division der SS 14/15 July 1944.

in a fiasco. With no contact with the units on its left or right, the regiment was decimated by heavy enemy artillery fire and constant air attacks before the attack developed. Not until the other grenadier regiments intervened was it possible to stabilize the front between Holubica and Kruhov. On 15 July 1944 the *Wehrmacht* communiqué announced:

> "*In the southern sector of the Eastern Front the Bolsheviks launched their anticipated attack in the area between Ternopol and Luck. This was repulsed yesterday in heavy fighting with the destruction of many tanks, individual penetrations were sealed off.*"

Former *Waffen-Grenadier* Michael Werkalec (*13./Waffen-Grenadier-Regiment der SS 29*) remembered:

> "*I was born in Carpathian Ukraine in 1922. When the German Wehrmacht reached the Ukraine in 1941, many young people were recruited to work in the German war industry. When the number of volunteers proved insufficient, regular deportations began. Many fled and hid in the forest, and finally the UPA was formed. As this had few weapons, our leaders told us to join the Galicia Division. Let yourself be trained and armed. One day we will need you.*
> *So in early 1943, after a medical examination, I arrived at the Heidelager camp. We were transferred for special training: I was sent to Mühlhausen in Alsace—others to Holland or the Protectorate of Bohemia and Moravia. After about two months I returned to the division, which by then was in Neuhammer on the Queiss.*
> *Orders for transfer to the front came at the end of May-first of June 1944. Waffen-Grenadier-Regiment der SS 30 was completely destroyed at the front in two hours, after the German units it was supposed to relieve had already abandoned their positions. The regiment marched to its destruction completely unawares.*
> *I had been the best rifle shot in training. I didn't fire a single shot at the front as I was soon wounded—before the pocket formed. By the time I rejoined the division it was already in Slovakia.*"

While *Waffen-Grenadier-Regiment der SS 29* and *31* were engaged in fierce fighting, the shattered *Waffen-Grenadier-Regiment der SS 30* was pulled out of the front line, reorganized, and elements committed against enemy troops that had broken through. On 16 July the *Wehrmacht* High Command announced:

> "*In the Ternopol and Lutsk combat zones our divisions repulsed the Bolshevik attacks, which were supported by powerful armored forces. Counterattacks eliminated or reduced a number of penetrations with the destruction of many tanks.*"

In the north, on 17 July the Red Army advanced in a wide arc through Radziechow south in the direction of Busk, and from the Zborov area to Zloczow. Of course, the *Wehrmacht* communiqué said nothing about the imminent encirclement of large German units:

> "*In the southern sector of the Eastern Front the defensive struggle east of the Upper Bug grew in intensity. Soviet armored forces attacking from the area of Ternopol and Lutsk were*

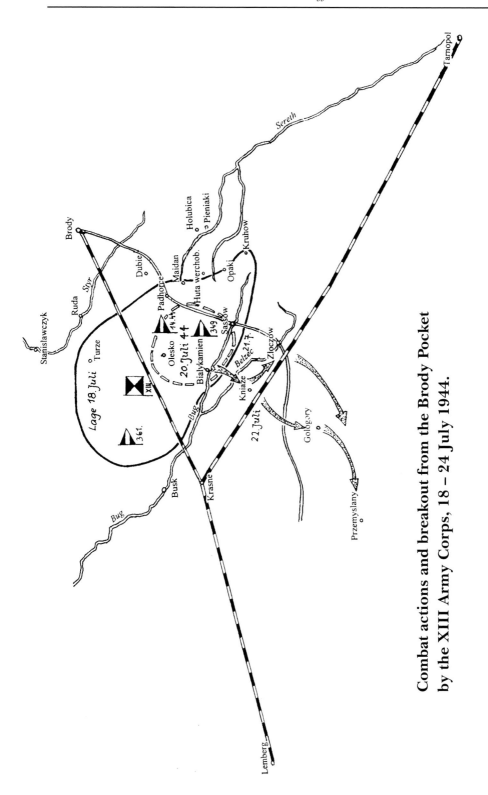

**Combat actions and breakout from the Brody Pocket
by the XIII Army Corps, 18 – 24 July 1944.**

halted in heavy back-and-forth fighting. 125 enemy tanks were destroyed there in both of the last two days."

On 18 July 1944, in summer temperatures, the Soviet armored spearheads linked up near Busk, trapping large elements of the XIII Army Corps in the Busk—Turze—Padhorce—Maidan—Opaki—Kruhov—Kniaze area. The seriousness of the situation could be read between the lines of the *Wehrmacht* communiqué:

"In the southern sector of the Eastern Front the fury of the enemy's attacks grew, especially east of the Upper Bug. There heavy fighting raged against enemy forces attacking in the direction of Lvov. 431 Soviet tanks have been destroyed there since 14 July."

The Ukrainian SS units were deployed on the hills east of the Padhorce—Zloczow road. As a result of heavy artillery fire and air attacks, the individual companies lost contact with each other and often had to fight on their own. Within two days forceful armored attacks had reduced the pocket to the area of Olesko—Bialykamien—Sasov. In this apocalyptic situation no one was able to care for the wounded and fallen—the field hospital of the *14. Waffen-Grenadier-Division der SS (galizische Nr. 1)*, with about 400 German and Ukrainian wounded, remained behind in Konty, near Padhorce. In this hopeless situation many desperate men committed suicide. A relief force from the west, the 8th Panzer Division and the 20th Panzer Grenadier Division, was forced to turn back, as Soviet forces were already at the gates of Lvov. The corps received authorization to abandon its positions and break out to the west. On 20 July 1944 the *Wehrmacht* High Command announced:

"On the Eastern Front, our divisions in the Lvov area are engaged in fierce defensive fighting. Attempts by the enemy to break through in the direction of the city itself were thwarted."

Finally, at dawn on 21 July 1944, the surrounded elements of the XIII Army Corps assembled in a forest near Bialykamien. Under heavy enemy fire, the leading troops succeeded in smashing a 200-meter-wide (sic!) breach in the enemy's encircling front; however, the untested members of the *14. Waffen-Grenadier-Division der SS (galizische Nr. 1)* could not stand the strain of continuous artillery and tank fire and air attacks and pulled back again beyond Kniaze. That evening *SS-Brigadeführer* Freitag declared that he no longer had control over his division. The commanding general of the XIII Army Corps, *General der Infanterie* Arthur Hauffe, subsequently placed the remnants of the division under the commander of the 361st Infantry Division, *Generalmajor* Gerhard Lindemann.[27] *Generalleutnant* Lasch[28] committed his 349th Infantry Division in another attempt to break out, while *Generalmajor* Lindemann, with the two divisions now under his command, tried to maintain contact. The *Wehrmacht* communiqué of 21 July 1944 declared:

"In the east, fighting in the Lvov area and on the Upper Bug continues with undiminished intensity. Our divisions continue to put up fierce resistance against the Soviets and are inflicting heavy losses."

The next day, while attempting to advance further southwest across the Krasne—Ternopol railway line, *Generalmajor* Lindemann was captured by the Soviets. This left *SS-Brigadeführer* Freitag the highest-ranking officer among the remaining approximately 4,000 soldiers (remains of the 361st Infantry Division and the *14. Waffen-Grenadier-Division der SS*). Under continuous fire from enemy artillery and aircraft order broke down. While the first troops advanced directly from Kniaze to Gologory, the last fell back in the direction of Zloczow and tried to break out there.

Beyond the rail line there were huge fields of uncut grain. The soldiers first sought cover there and then tried to storm across a birch-covered plateau toward the southwest. Most of the vehicles and heavy weapons were gone, but in any case they would have been of little use in the difficult terrain. Erich Rommel was one of the German core personnel of *Waffen-Grenadier-Regiment der SS 29*:

"I volunteered for the Waffen-SS in 1942 and served with the 3rd SS Panzer Division Totenkopf, the 16th Panzer Grenadier Division Reichsführer-SS and the SS Special Purpose Training Battalion. Then in February 1944 I was sent to join the 14. Waffen-Grenadier-Division der SS (galizische Nr. 1) at Neuhammer on the Queiss.

There I became command post clerk in SS Volunteer Regiment 1 (later renamed Waffen-Grenadier-Regiment der SS 29) under SS-Standartenführer Dern. The adjutant was SS-Obersturmführer Ditze.

In June 1944 we were sent into action west of Ternopol in Galicia. Waffen-Grenadier-Regiment der SS 29 saw heavy action, especially from 17 to 21 July 1944 at Padhorce, Chwatow And Bialy-Kamin.

The division was wiped out in the pocket east of Brody and there was a visible decline in the previously strict order. In the end we were a mishmash of Wehrmacht, Luftwaffe and Waffen-SS without heavy weapons, with little ammunition and no air support.

On the morning of 17 July 1944 we were ordered to move the regimental command post to the rear. As we were drinking coffee in a farmhouse, we suddenly came under Russian fire from all sides. Acting quickly, we immediately returned fire. My friend Bauer was killed in this action. I used my submachine-gun to cover the withdrawal of our regimental commander and his adjutant. After disengaging from the Russians, we drove across a bridge, which was blown up soon afterwards as the river represented a natural obstacle. Up front SS-Obersturmbannführer Dern, the regimental commander, took over the leaderless 13th Company and ordered the anti-tank guns moved into position. To our dismay, masses of T-34 tanks appeared over the edge of the hollow in which we were situated.

We were surrounded and under continuous air attack. Throughout the day the commander's driver, SS-Unterscharführer Daumann, and I continuously called to one another to see if the other was still alive. Our newly-formed battle group made repeated attempts to break the pocket. At first our efforts were in vain. In a village full of wounded and laid-out Red Crosses my friend and I became separated when the Russian close-support aircraft shot everything to pieces. All of the wounded remained in the pocket. The road was clogged with vehicles and men, nothing moved.

On 18 July I was with an SS man from my division, a Ukrainian and a German Feldwebel. The Feldwebel had unlimited optimism, repeatedly telling me: 'We are definitely going to make it home, you just have to believe that!' As he climbed up a railway embankment to look for the enemy, he was struck by a burst of machine-gun fire and rolled down to my feet.

On 20 July I was lying in a wheat field with a group of others, shooting at individual Russians with a carbine, but they were quite far away. Then, suddenly, I felt something strike my right heel. I had been hit by a shell fragment. As we were under continuous fire, it seemed like quite a while until I received first aid. Then I moved on, wearing just my left boot as they had cut off the right one.

Then we lay for hours beside the road. Soviet armored cars came by at intervals, firing like mad. Luckily we were in a blind spot.

On the evening of 21 July some comrades and I got out of the pocket. In a small village we came upon many surrendered Red Army soldiers, some deserters and a badly-wounded Russian. He was lying on a wrecked anti-tank gun and he stretched both arms out to me: in one hand he had a packet of ruble notes, in the other a photo of his family. The stream was filled with dead, both our men and Red Army; we were so thirsty we drank the water anyway. In great distress, wounded horses screamed like humans."

On 23 July 1944, continuously in combat and under Russian fire, the men reached Przemyslany. The *Wehrmacht* High Command announced:

"In the east the defensive struggle continues with great ferocity. In the Lvov area enemy spearheads have reached the eastern edge of the city... Everywhere there our divisions are putting up fierce resistance against the advancing enemy."

On 24 July 1944 the soldiers successfully broke through and established contact with German forces. By way of Chodorow—Stryj—Drohobycz—Sambor—Turka—Uzsok, the survivors of the *14. Waffen-Grenadier-Division der SS (galizische Nr. 1)* reached the Carpathian-Ukraine in Hungary. The later *SS-Obersturmführer* Bernhard Dornbusch recalled:

"Commanding the Heavy Company of SS Field Replacement Battalion 14 was an SS-Obersturmführer Schneller. On the day of the Soviet breakthrough there was an alarm. We saw the Russians advancing west on the parallel road—in no time SS-Obersturmführer Schneller was gone!

As the next in rank I had to lead the company. There were just two German and two Ukrainian NCOs—the rest were Ukrainian enlisted men. One could even converse in German with those of them who were students. We were in Besbrody near Busk and had no contact with the enemy during the encirclement.

My successor as adjutant of II./Waffen-Grenadier-Regiment der SS 29 was killed by a direct hit on the command post near Brody—the battalion commander was also missing from that time on.

After the breakout SS Field Replacement Battalion 14 was transported by rail back to Neuhammer under its commander, SS-Sturmbannführer Kleinow. I had orders to carry out an overland march with weapons and equipment. As soon as rail transport became available, we were also to proceed to Neuhammer. I made it to Sanok, where I was assigned to the military commander, Knight's Cross wearer Oberst von Künsberg.[29] I led two companies in his 'Carpathian Regiments' until I was ordered to Neuhammer for reformation."

After a year in the formation process the division had been shattered in just 10 days. The unit had marched to the front with about 11,000 members; of these only about 3,000 made it back to the German lines. The missing 8,000 Ukrainian men had been killed, captured by the enemy, or were hiding among the Ukrainian population. Some of the latter also made contact with the UPA. Because of the chaotic conditions during the encirclement and the breakout attempts it was often impossible to determine who of the missing had been killed, captured, or separated from the unit. The division pharmacist, *SS-Hauptsturmführer* Werner Beneke, wrote this to the wife of a missing German *SS-Unterarzt*:

"*My dearest madam.*

You will perhaps have already learned that our division was encircled in the Brody combat zone. Elements of the division fought their way out and are assembling at our former post, the Neuhammer training camp. Reports are coming in daily of comrades with other units, especially from hospitals they are in. Some of the reports are already very old, which is due to slowness of the mail from the front. I am therefore turning to you today to ask if you can tell us anything of your husband, about whom unfortunately we have so far received no news. As soon as we receive any news we will inform you immediately. In the hope that we will soon be in possession of positive news about our universally-liked comrade, I remain with best wishes!"

For the fighting in the Brody pocket, *Generalleutnant* Otto Lasch and *Generalmajor* Gerhard Lindemann were awarded the Knight's Cross with Oak Leaves on 10 September 1944. *SS-Brigadeführer* Fritz Freitag was awarded the Knight's Cross of the Iron Cross on 30 September 1944.[30] Himmler showed his opinion of the Ukrainian volunteers after receiving a biased report by the division commander.[31] He did not mention that Freitag had lost his nerve on 21 July 1944 and simply laid down command of the division:

"*SS-Brigadeführer Freitag displayed extraordinary personal courage in commanding his division under uniquely difficult conditions in the Brody pocket.*

His division was not made up of German soldiers prepared to give their all, but of Ukrainians from Galicia, psychologically weak and inconstant, to whom the manly and military German virtues are foreign.

Maintaining control of and commanding such men, inexperienced in combat and lacking toughness, while carrying out the most difficult order—combat in the Brody pocket—demanded the utmost and unique effort on the part of the responsible officer.

The first impression of combat gained by the division, which conditions placed at the decisive point of the fighting in the pocket as of 12/7/1944, was that of retreating German units.

When it appeared that the reinforced Grenadier-Regiment 30 might be drawn into this retreat, it was the division commander with the regimental commander who acted on the spot to stabilize the situation in that sector and prevent an imminent breakthrough.

When, during the subsequent course of the battle, numerous volunteers fled from sheer cowardice and in some cases turned their weapons on their own officers and NCOs, once again it was the division commander to a decisive degree who unhesitatingly took action on the spot to restore the situation and employ the necessary brutal measures against these wretches.[32]

The division carried out its mission under the most difficult conditions until 19/7/1944. This was achieved with Ukrainians, who with few exceptions were not fighters, supported by just a handful of German personnel.[33]

That the division, committed at the focal point of the battle, was able to achieve this acknowledged success, is due solely to the German officers, led by their division commander. To a decisive degree it rests on their personal actions at the critical points of the battle.

The tragedy in the division's action is that it was denied a decisive success despite the exemplary behavior of the division commander."

April 1944: inspecting the division at the Neuhammer SS training camp.

Behind left: *SS-Brigadeführer* **Dr. Wächter**
behind right: *SS-Brigadeführer* **Freitag**
front left: *Oberst* **Bysanz, head of the Ukrainian Military Board**

Division inspection in April 1944.

SS-Brigadeführer **Freitag and the operations officer** *SS-Sturmbannführer* **Heike.**

Soldiers setting up communications equipment.

The 81.4-mm mortar used by the heavy companies.

Digging a foxhole.

A medium anti-aircraft gun.

The 14ᵗʰ SS Division's headquarters building in Neuhammer.

Address by Freitag during Himmler's visit on 16 May 1944.

Freiwilligen-Hauptsturmführer **Paliyev translates the speech.**

From l. to r.: *Oberst* Bysanz, *SS-Brigadeführer* Dr. Wächter, and *SS-Sturmbannführer* Heike.

Dr. Wächter's speech to officers of the division and Himmler on 16 May 1944.

SS-Brigadeführer Freitag in conversation with German officers.

SS-Sturmbannführer **Heike (left) in conversation with officers.**

Reformation

On 7 August 1944 Himmler sent a telex from his field headquarters to the chief of the SS-FHA, *SS-Obergruppenführer* Jüttner,[34] ordering the reformation of the *14. Waffen-Grenadier-Division der SS (galiz. Nr. 1)* at the Neuhammer training camp in Silesia.[35] Acting on this, on 5 September the SS-FHA issued orders for the division to be reestablished.[36] Forming the core of the division were the 3rd battalions of the three grenadier regiments formed by the 14th SS Waffen Grenadier Replacement Training Regiment by order of the SS-FHA.[37]

SS-Brigadeführer Freitag, who was against reformation and rejected another command of the division, was ordered to continue in command by Himmler "*on account of his acquired experience.*" His obvious inability and his disinterest in leading this foreign unit were disregarded because of the unavailability of another possible division commander.

Soon afterwards the first Ukrainians who had escaped the pocket began arriving in Neuhammer from northern Hungary. As the camp was overcrowded, they initially had to be quartered in a former POW camp. Shortages in personnel were immediately made good by the 14th SS Waffen Grenadier Replacement Training Regiment, which had been transferred from Wandern to Neuhammer. As a result of incorporating the 4th and 5th Galician volunteer Regiments the unit had a strength of approximately 8,000 men.[38] Consequently, on 20 September 1944 the division was already able to boast a complement of:

Officers	NCOs	Enlisted Men	Total
261	673	11,967	12,901 actual
2%	5.2%	92.8%	100%
480	2,587	11,682	14,749 authorized
3.3%	17.5%	79.2%	100%

A comparison between authorized and actual strengths once again reveals major shortfalls in officers and NCOs, though sufficient numbers of enlisted men were available.[39] Eventually, it would have been possible to make up this shortfall with Ukrainians, but *SS-Brigadeführer* Freitag rejected the idea—he wanted an officer and NCO corps that was as exclusively German as possible. Thus, the division was not operational.

Action in Slovakia

On 23 August 1944 the Slovakian National Uprising broke out under the command of the Slovakian Defense Minister General Catlos. On 19 September the *14. Waffen-Grenadier-Division der SS* received orders to form a battle group equivalent in strength to a reinforced battalion, in order to support German troops in Slovakia. The force was formed under the command of *SS-Obersturmbannführer* Karl Wildner three days later and consisted of:

- *III./ 14. Waffen-Grenadier-Regiment der SS 29*
- a light battery of *Waffen-Artillerie-Regiment der SS 14*
- two platoons from SS Anti-Tank Battalion 14
- two pioneer platoons
- elements of SS Signals Battalion 14
- elements of SS Waffen Supply Regiment 14

SS Battle Group Wildner was subsequently transported from the Neuhammer training camp to Slovakia on three transport trains. The transports eventually arrived in the Zemlianske Kostolany area, where the troops were attached to SS Battle Group Schill, with which it was to engage Slovakian rebels in Königsberg (Nova Bania).

At the same time the SS-FHA also ordered the transfer of the *14. Waffen-Grenadier-Division der SS* and the 14th SS Waffen Grenadier Replacement Training Regiment into the Slovakian protective zone to put an end to the uprising there.[41] Former *Waffen-Grenadier* B.S. recalled:

"A Ukrainian student, in August 1941 in Vienna I volunteered for the Galician Division. At the Neuhammer training camp I was issued a uniform and assigned to 11th Company/14th SS Waffen Grenadier Replacement Training Regiment. My company commander was SS-Oberscharführer Josef Radl from the Sudetenland. On 20 April 1945 he was promoted to SS-Untersturmführer. My battalion commander was SS-Hauptsturmführer Wilhelm Schram. He came from the Leibstandarte Adolf Hitler, as indicated by a stripe on his sleeve. He was also promoted on Hitler's birthday, to SS-Sturmbannführer.

At the end of September 1944 we left Neuhammer for Slovakia. There we were given additional training and took part in minor actions. Fortunately there was no contact with the enemy, either in Slovakia or Slovenia."

On 2 October 1944 SS Battle Group Wildner proceeded to Hochwiesen (Vel'ke Pole) and Königsberg (Nova Bana) via Oslany. There was fighting near Zarnovica and Heiligenkreuz (Sväty Kriz). On 9 October the battle group was engaged near Banska Stiavnica and Schemnitz. In the middle of the month the Ukrainians advanced through Altsohl (Zvolen) to Neusohl (Banka Bystrica).

On 7 October 1944 *SS-Brigadeführer* Freitag drove via Vienna to Bratislava to discuss employment of the division with *SS-Obergruppenführer* Höfle.[42] As the division was not yet again fit for operations, with the exception of SS Battle Group Wildner it was only capable of performing security duties.

Höfle subsequently made the division responsible for security in the area surrounding Sillein. The *14. Division* was to relieve the Tatra Division, which was moving out of the area to attack Banska Bystrica, the center of resistance. The next day Freitag made his way to Sillein to meet with *Generalleutnant* von Loeper,[43] commander of the Tatra Division, and discuss the takeover of the area. The Ukrainians would secure the area Cadca – Bela – Sv. Martin – Rajec – V. Bytca. Through this area ran the important rail lines from Upper Silesia to Pressburg (Bratislava) and from Sillein (Zilina) to Rosenberg (Ruzemberok).

While from 10 to 18 October 1944 Höfle assembled the available German troops to end the Slovakian National Uprising, on 15 October the transfer of the Ukrainians from Neuhammer into the designated area began, with the division headquarters occupying quarters in Sillein.

At the same time Freitag received orders to form a second battle group. Commanded by *SS-Sturmbannführer* Friedrich Wittenmeyer, the unit consisted of the reinforced *II./Waffen-Grenadier-Regiment der SS 30*. On 17 October SS Battle Group Wittenmeyer arrived in the area around Deutschendorf – Neudorf by way of Sillein. In preparation for the coming operation elements of SS Special Regiment Dirlewanger[44] were attached to the battle group.

Barely two months after the start of the uprising, on 18 October 1944 Höfle gave the order for a concentric attack against the Slovakian rebels. SS Battle Group Wildner returned to the division in Sillein, while SS Battle Group Wittenmeyer, with the attached convict soldiers of the Dirlewanger Regiment, took part in the attack from Vernar toward Neusohl (Banska Bystrica) until 31 October. A third battle group marched with little fighting from Rosenberg to Korytnica, in the Lower Tatra. By 15 November the area had been secured by the two battle groups, and remnants of the rebel army were being pursued into the Upper and Lower Tatra.

In December 1944 the division was tasked with strengthening various defensive positions; for example, on the Waag, near Sillein, and in the Nitra position from Sv. Martin through Vrutky in a northerly direction. With the end of the uprising the division was officially considered operational again. Three battle groups were now formed, each equivalent in strength to a reinforced grenadier regiment. One of these saw action in the Schemnitz area by order of Army Group South.

Fighting on the right wing of the 2nd Ukrainian Front, the Soviet 40th Army had crossed the Hungarian-Slovakian border by way of Belassagyarmat and Ipolysag.[45] The battle group of the *14. Waffen-Grenadier-Division der SS* was sent to Army Group Wöhler and joined combat at the end of December when Soviet troops advanced through Leva towards Königsberg and Schemnitz. After tough defensive fighting in the Schemnitz area, in January 1945 the reinforced regiment was sent back to the division.

The then *SS-Unterscharführer* Ludwig Hümmer (14th SS Medical Battalion) recalled of Christmas 1944:

"I had been a member of the 14th SS Waffen Grenadier Division since late summer 1944, at which time I went to the Neuhammer training camp for the reformation [of the division]. When I reported to the medical battalion there I was initially assigned to the office

with Karl Friedrich, then senior NCO, who came from Thuringia. Our first task was the sad one of notifying the families of the men who had been killed. As time went on the big fellow—he was almost two meters tall—and I became best friends And we complemented each other in almost every way, especially as I had been senior NCO in the SS Medical Battalion attached to Supply Command Center in Bobruisk in 1943. Later I saw action with a commando unit that was almost completely wiped out and as a result I was transferred to the 14th SS Division.

After having served with the Deutschland Regiment, I had misgivings about joining such a unit. But I soon came to realize what unique comrades these all were. I am speaking here of the Ukrainians—there were only a few of us Germans. There were many students in our battalion—I remember my comrade Hladinand Bych, but also former enlisted men from the Red Army.

From Neuhammer we were moved into Slovakia to Sillein (Zilina). Our battalion was quartered on the outskirts of the town, out by a cellulose factory, not far from the Waag. The impressive mountains of the High Tatra could be seen in the distance. Except for a few officers and NCOs the battalion consisted entirely of Ukrainians. Our duties were the same as in garrison and the training of the new recruits, equipped with completely new and first class equipment, continued. When possible the men went into town, seeking diversion in the relatively plentiful bars and cafes. One could also watch a movie in the theater—though most were in French with Czech subtitles.

Christmastime was approaching. As our Ukrainian comrades did not celebrate the holiday until January 6th, as is the custom in their country, on 24 December we Germans were one big family. Consequently a small gift was prepared for each one of us, and with the approval of the administrative officer, SS-Obersturmführer Dirksheide, special food and drink was also procured. The land of the High Tatra was covered in snow and big flakes were still falling when, toward evening, we trudged through the deep snow toward our blockhouses. We sat at the festively-decorated table, before us the Christmas tree, its candles lighting the small room, the gifts (letters and packages held back by the senior NCO), and the other things provided by our battalion. The candles provided the only light in the room as our commander, SS-Sturmbannführer Dr. Schmitt, spoke to us.

Then we had an experience which I have not forgotten to this day: a choir outside the blockhouse—[singing] a melancholy Ukrainian Christmas carol! Deep silence filled the room and we listened to the melody of the song that our Ukrainian comrades were singing to us. It was the most beautiful gift of that night. One of the men gently opened a window, and the deep voices sounded more clearly in our ears, like tolling bells. A few snowflakes blew in and quickly melted into nothing. The heavy snow had stopped though, scattered patches of cloud drifted in the firmament, and a few stars shone down on the seemingly peaceful winter night. Then the door opened, and a delegation of our Ukrainian SS men, covered in snow, came in to convey best wishes for our celebration on behalf of their comrades. They were warmly welcomed into our small circle and hugged. The experience of this night brought tears to the eyes of my comrades."

Ukrainian Waffen-Grenadier.

Ukrainian soldiers at the infantry gun school in Breslau-Lissa, Christmas 1944.

Serving an infantry gun.

Ukrainian *Waffen-Sturmmann* (1945 in Slovakia).

Waffen-Unterscharführer.

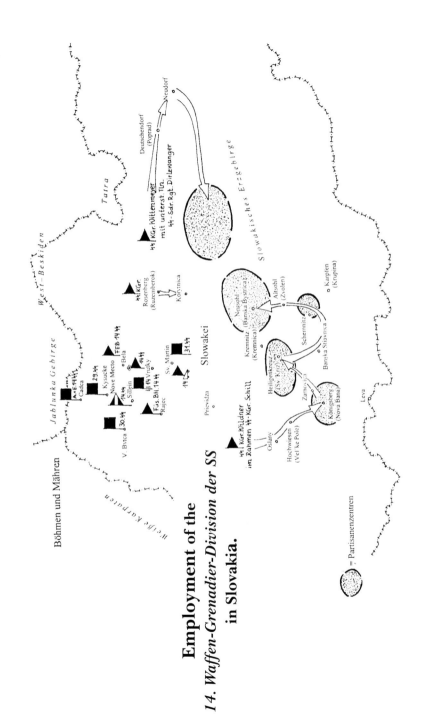

**Employment of the
14. Waffen-Grenadier-Division der SS
in Slovakia.**

Ukrainian Soldiers in Action with the 5. SS-Panzer-Division Wiking

On 23 March 1943 the SS-FHA ordered that the I Battalion of the Estonian Legion should be attached to the *SS-Panzergrenadier-Division Wiking*. The Estonians remained with the *SS-Panzergrenadier-Regiment Westland* as its III Battalion until about May 1944. They subsequently formed the SS Fusilier Battalion of the 20th Estonian SS Volunteer Division.

As replacements for the Estonians, it was decided that about 1,000 Ukrainian volunteers should join the formation, now designated 5. *SS-Panzer-Division Wiking*. Together with German recruits, a large percentage of the Ukrainians were used in the reformation of III Battalion/SS Panzer-Grenadier Regiment 10 Westland in the Protectorate of Bohemia and Moravia.[46] At the end of September 1944, when the battalion was sent to the 5. *SS-Panzer-Division* in the area around Nieporent between the Narev and Vistula Rivers, the division, part of the newly-formed *IV. SS-Panzer-Korps*, along with the 3. *SS-Panzer-Division Totenkopf*, had already fought the first two defensive battles of Warsaw.[47]

On 10 October 1944, following a two-hour artillery barrage, the enemy once again attacked the *IV. SS-Panzer-Korps*, in the sector of the front between the Vistula and the Narev. The *Wehrmacht* High Command announced:

"After heavy artillery fire the Bolsheviks launched fierce attacks north of Warsaw and south of Rozan. For the most part they were repulsed, immediate counterattacks eliminated or reduced penetrations."

There was fierce fighting, which by 15 October 1944 had cost *IV. SS-Panzer-Korps* 5,000 casualties. On that day the *Wehrmacht* communiqué declared:

"In heavy fighting yesterday our troops again achieved defensive successes north of Warsaw and in the two Narev bridgeheads at Seroc and Rozan. Despite the massed use of tanks, artillery and aircraft, nowhere did the Bolsheviks achieved their desired breakthrough."

On 28 October of that year the Red Army halted its major attacks in that sector of the front. It had committed almost three entire armies in this third battle northwest of the Polish capital. The 5. *SS-Panzer-Division*, with *SS-Panzergrenadier-Regiment 10*, remained in position in an again shortened line east of Nowy Dwor in the so-called "Wet Triangle" between the Narev and the Vistula, while *SS-Panzergrenadier-Regiment 9 Germania* was attached to the 542. *Volksgrenadier-Division* north of the Bug. The *Wehrmacht* High Command declared:

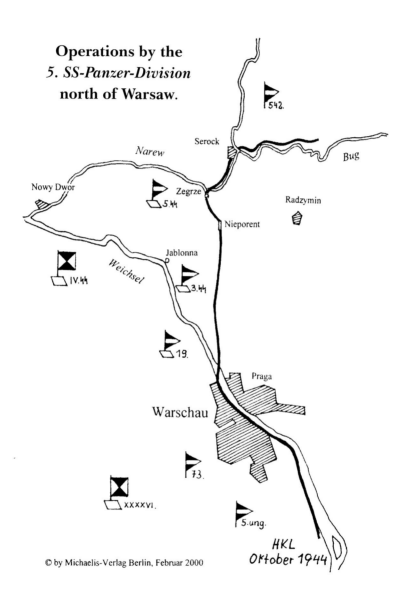

Operations by the
5. SS-Panzer-Division
north of Warsaw.

542.

Narew

Serock

Bug

Nowy Dwor

Zegrze

5.ᴴ

Radzymin

Nieporent

Weichsel

Jablonna

3.ᴴ

IV.ᴴ

19.

Praga

Warschau

73.

XXXXVI.

5.ung.

HKL
Oktober 1944

"*Local attacks by the Bolsheviks between Warsaw and the Bug collapsed.*"

The former *Waffen-Grenadier* Ostap Hladkiwskyj (*11./SS-Panzergrenadier-Regiment 10* Westland) recalled:

"*I was born in Galicia on 15 May 1926. The Ukrainians suffered a great deal under Polish rule. My father, who was employed by the Polish state, had to convert from the Greek-Catholic to the Roman-Catholic faith in order to keep his job.*

When the Soviets came, many nationalists were imprisoned. Thus the German Wehrmacht was greeted with flowers as a real liberator. When conditions did not change, however—the shops were empty under the Soviets and stayed that way under the Germans, disillusionment slowly began to set in.

Young Ukrainians were initially drafted into the construction service for two years. Poor food and hard work led to rising resistance. Finally the police began simply snatching young people from the schools and even train stations and deporting them to Germany to work. People began to hate the Germans.

Then suddenly in 1943 we began hearing the slogan urging us to fight for a new Europe in an SS Galician Volunteer Division. Many were attracted by recruiting posters depicting young SS men and pretty girls.

In February 1944 the Russians advanced toward our village but were thrown back by the Germans. This caused us young people from the village to talk about joining the division.

In June 1944 all men between 16 and 36 were rounded up. In the labor service one could decide whether to go to Germany to work or take up arms. Many went to Germany to get as far away from the Russians as possible.

I and about 30 others joined the SS division and our departure was celebrated with flowers and singing. On the way to the station, however, some had a change of heart and abruptly disappeared into house entrances or side streets… In Lvov we underwent a medical examination and were sent by train in civilian clothes to Kirchbaum near Neuhammer.

There 1,000 men were initially selected and sent to Camp Heidelager. Finally we arrived in the Seltschan area in the Protectorate of Bohemia and Moravia. Together with Ukrainian and German comrades I was assigned to the 11th Company of SS-Panzergrenadier-Regiment 10 Westland.

Instead of laced shoes we were issued proper hobnailed boots and better uniforms. The collar patch with the lion remained, however, as did the rank designation Waffen-Grenadier. This disparagement compared to our German comrades, who were designated SS-Panzergrenadiere, already angered us.

There were serious language difficulties during training, and so we simply imitated what the others did. In September 1944 we were taken in trucks to the station and from there sent by train to Modlin, where the 5. SS-Panzer-Division Wiking was situated. We now knew that we were about to see action at the front and we were afraid. At first we manned a second line and there suffered our first casualties to Soviet snipers.

Then on 10 October 1944 all hell broke loose. We came under fire from artillery and Stalin Organs, and then masses of tanks approached. They overran us and we had to fight our way back in small groups. Especially awful for me was the fate of my German comrade and friend Paul. He was wounded in both legs and could not walk. I picked him up and carried him on my shoulders—but neither he had the strength to hold on for long nor I to carry him back to the German lines. The others repeatedly shouted to me: quick, quick. Come on! With a heavy heart I had to put him down. Finally we reached some of our tanks and were saved. Just 12 men survived from my company. Of the 26 Ukrainians in the company there were only three—one of them me.

Soon afterwards it was announced that all the Ukrainians were to assemble for transfer to the 14. Waffen-Grenadier-Division der SS. Of the original 1,000 men just 300 were left. The rest had been killed, wounded or taken prisoner."

Former *Waffen-Grenadier* Anton Hrycszyn was also attached to the *Wiking* Division. He recalled:

"Soon after we arrived in Kirchbaum, SS-Sturmbannführer Rusnak appeared again and told us that there weren't enough Ukrainian officers for our training. Fortunately, he said, the famous 5. SS-Panzer-Division Wiking had already indicated its willingness to train 1,000 recruits. These had to pass another physical examination, however, and meet a minimum height requirement. Rusnak promised us that these men would only be sent for training and would later be sent back to the Galician Division.

I was accepted, but unlike the most of us I was sent to a supply company instead of the SS-Regiment Westland. One day the German and Ukrainian soldiers were formed into two lines and the NCOs formed groups, each of two Germans and two Ukrainians, which were to share a tent. We weren't very happy about that, for on the one hand it made us Ukrainians feel like we were being watched, and we could hardly converse with the Germans. Anyway everyone preferred to spend as much time as possible with his own countrymen. Sometimes there even brawls between we Ukrainians and the Germans. In my tent was a young student from Essen who told me that had not joined the Waffen-SS voluntarily but had been drafted. I felt rather sorry for him, for it seemed that he came from a good home and now had to share a tent with us young farmers.

One day we were moved to the Heidelager training camp, which was deep in the forest. Our NCO was a German and had difficulty making himself understood. Finally I was appointed interpreter. During our first conversations I discovered that he was from Silesia and spoke Polish. I told him that we Ukrainians from Galicia understood Polish and this made everything simpler.

Then we were taken by train to Strasice, where we received additional training. It was probably September 1944 when we were entrained again. We were at least sure that we weren't going to the front, as Rusnak had promised us that we would only be trained in the Wiking Division. When we arrived in Poland we could see columns of smoke and dust everywhere on the horizon—we were at the front. We occupied southwards-facing positions on the Narev to prevent the Red Army from breaking into East Prussia.

We remained on the Narev with no heavy weapons for about a week and then heard that the Russians had broken through on our left. We were subsequently moved to Modlin, which was probably being used as a sort of distribution point for the troops at the front. Soon afterwards we received orders to proceed to the Pushka Kampinovska Forest near Warsaw to hunt partisans. For this task we formed a skirmish line with about 10 meters between each other and walked through the forest. In a small settlement we found roasted potatoes still warm—the partisans had thus left a short time before and were avoiding any contact with us.

Another time we were supposed to evacuate the surrounding villages as the Red Army was advancing steadily. The inhabitants were given just half an hour to pack their belongings. After these actions we returned to Modlin and from there to the front. Our supply company was now looking for co-drivers for the trucks. Figuring that driving was better than walking, I immediately volunteered. There were four Ukrainian co-drivers altogether: Fedoriv, Yatsek, Mel'nyk and I. Yatsek and Mel'nyk were former Red Army men from the East Ukraine who had been taken prisoner. My driver was a fatherly, nice Dutchman, with whom I now transported artillery ammunition.

We then had several days of rest and were quartered in a wood. There we were joined by an NCO who was very friendly and who was always laughing and cracking jokes. He asked us where we all came from—w were mainly Ukrainians in this supply company. When I told him I had been in Ternopol, he told me that he had been present at the shooting of Jews there…

Soon afterwards an alert company was formed—I was included and had to say farewell to my Dutch comrade. During the night we were supposed to dig two-man foxholes next to a railway line. As we worked we were fired on by the enemy. There was shooting from every direction. I was so panic-stricken that I immediately broke off the handle of my shovel and had to continue digging with my hands. Finally we crawled into our foxhole and waited for morning, hoping that it would be better. When we saw what we were facing, we prayed for night to come again. When we no longer saw anyone to the left or right, Fedoriv and I left the foxhole and ran into the forest behind us. There were military police there, and they shouted that we should return to our positions. They had already been taken by the enemy and the order was given to fix bayonets and prepare to attack.

I no longer know how, but we retook our positions and were even able to capture a few Red Army men. There were several wounded lying about and Fedoriv and I took them to the rear.

The nervous strain was enormous and we Ukrainians knew that the alternative of surrendering and being taken prisoner would surely have meant death for us as collaborators wearing the uniform of the Waffen-SS. After much discussion, Fedoriv and I agreed to shoot one another in the foot or shoulder. Of course we knew full well what that might possibly entail. Another possibility, which some of us turned to, was to don civilian clothes and go into the Polish underground. But I didn't trust the Poles and decided on the first-named. Finally I used my rifle as a crutch and after a few days landed in a military hospital in Reichenberg, where I even received the Wound Badge in Black."

As it was turning out that the men were not only being trained by the 5. SS-*Division*—as originally promised—but would also be deployed at the front for a long time, on 24 October 1944 the head of the Military Board of Galicia wrote:

"The SS-Division Wiking took in a thousand Ukrainian volunteers from Galicia from the replacement regiment of the 14th SS Waffen Grenadier Division (Galician No. 1). Insurmountable difficulties could arise, because these volunteers joined the Galicia Division, not the Wiking Division. For example, in the Galicia Division it is possible for Ukrainian-speaking volunteers to become NCOs and officers, provided they have completed the course and have the required experience. There the volunteers also attend mass and receive propaganda in their mother tongue, which gives those who have not served before the necessary stability and the moral strength to fulfill their duties and obligations.

I ask that you give SS-Obersturmführer Habrusewydz, who is to be chaplain for the Ukrainian volunteers in the Wiking Division, the opportunity to give special attention to the volunteers. In letters to their families and to the military board, many of them have complained that they can't understand why the aren't serving in the Galicia Division and that, as mentioned above, the promises made to them during recruitment have not been kept. I wish to point out that serious consequences could arise from this dissatisfaction and the lack of understanding of these young volunteers combined with their inability to discuss the situation with their NCOs and officers...”

The situation soon eased, however, when the SS-FHA ordered the Ukrainian volunteers back to the *14. Waffen-Grenadier-Division der SS.* On 4 November 1944 the commander of the *5. SS-Panzer-Division Wiking, SS-Standartenführer* Ullrich,[48] bade farewell to the Ukrainian soldiers:

"Volunteer fighters against bolshevism!
Three weeks of fierce fighting lay behind us. You have, each in his place, done your duty, thereby helping to hold the front against an enemy superior in numbers.
The Reichsführer-SS has now ordered your release by the division and return to the Galician SS Volunteer Division.
I thank you for the will to fight against bolshevism that you have demonstrated and wish you continued good luck in the ranks of the Galician SS Volunteer Division until the final victory over our mortal enemy bolshevism.”

Ostap Hladkiwskyj

Erich Rommel with his driver Daumann in regimental commander Dern's Schwimmwagen.

**Short rest during the move from Slovakia to Slovenia
in February 1945.**

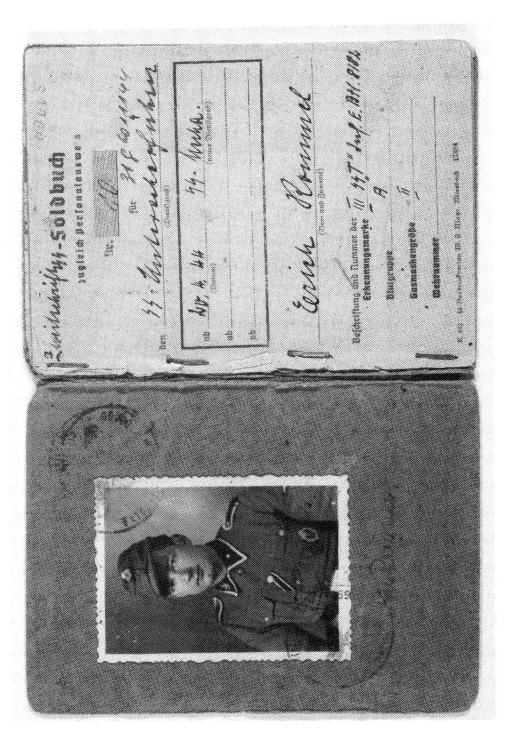

Erich Rommel's paybook (Soldbuch).

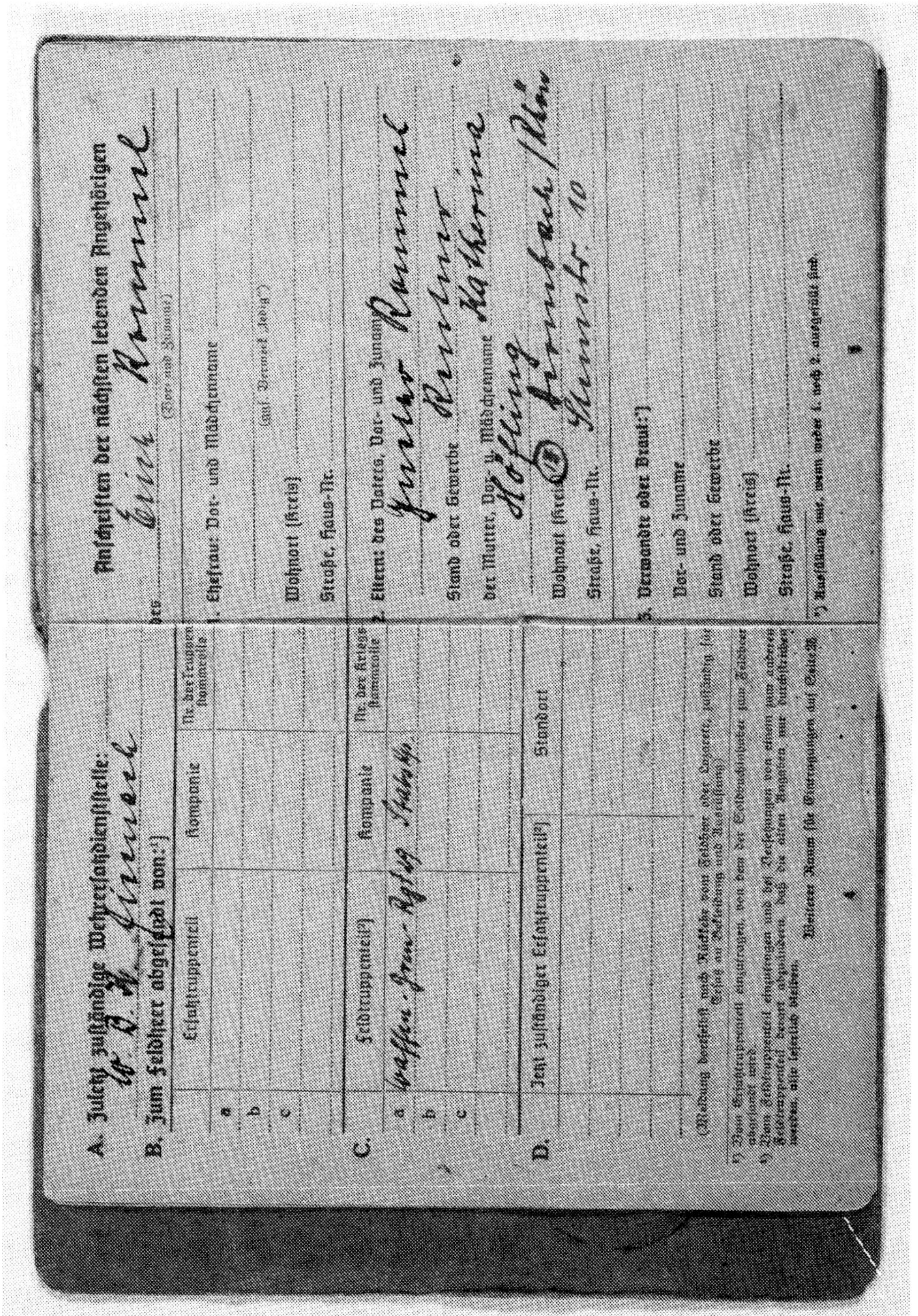

A. Zuletzt zuständige Wehrersatzdienststelle:

B. Zum Feldheer abgesandt von:¹)

	Ersatztruppenteil	Kompanie	Nr. der Truppen-Stammrolle
a			
b			
c			

C.

	Feldtruppenteil²)	Kompanie	Nr. der Kriegs-Stammrolle
a	Waffen-Gren.-Rgt.		
b			
c			

D.

Jetzt zuständiger Ersatztruppenteil²)	Standort

Anschriften der nächsten lebenden Angehörigen

(Vor- und Zuname)

1. Ehefrau: Vor- und Mädchenname

(auf Vermerk ledig*)

Wohnort (Kreis)

Straße, Haus-Nr.

2. Eltern: des Vaters, Vor- und Zuname

Stand oder Gewerbe

der Mutter, Vor- u. Mädchenname Katharina

Wohnort (Kreis)

Straße, Haus-Nr. 10

3. Verwandte oder Braut:¹)

Vor- und Zuname

Stand oder Gewerbe

Wohnort (Kreis)

Straße, Haus-Nr.

*) Ausfüllung nur, wenn unter 1. und 2. ausgefüllt sind.

Nachweisung über eine etwaige Aufnahme in ein Standort-, Feld-, Kriegs- oder Reservelazarett

Lazarett:	Tag und Monat	Jahr	Krankheit	Unterschrift des abgebenden Truppenteils (Kompaniem usw. Oberfeldwebel)	Tag und Monat	Jahr	Etwaige Bemerkung in Bezug auf die Entlassung aus dem Lazarett (übergeführt nach TRL als erholt zum Truppenteil usw.)	Unterschrift des die Entlassung bewirkenden Lazarettbeamten
	der Laz.-Aufnahme				bei Entlassung aus dem Lazarett			
Kriegslazarett 1695	28.7.	1944	Gr. Granatsplitter re. Kopf	./.	8.9.	44	Heil Laz. Zug. Zug gez.	gez. Unterschrift
Res. Lazarett Bed Hall	15.9.	1944	"	./.	10.11.	44	"	"
bei der Truppe	20.7.	1944	Gr. Splitter li. Oberschenkel				T.U.P.v.v.H.	
							Oberarzt u. Chefarzt W. Winter im Res. Laz.	
						44		
					6.4.	45	Truppe	

21

LNch 22 | 1943 | 44 | Allerschnellstens | | | | | |
| 15000 e | 30.3. | 44 | -25- | | | | | |

20

Mitgegebene Wertsachen und Papiere siehe folgende Seite!

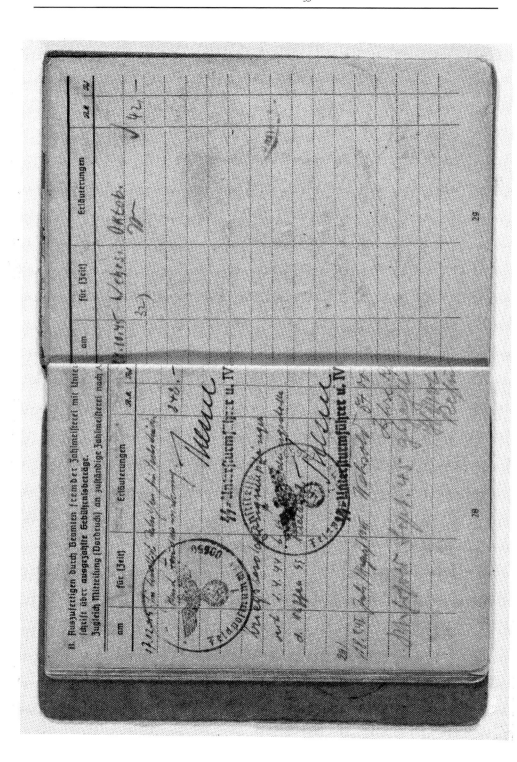

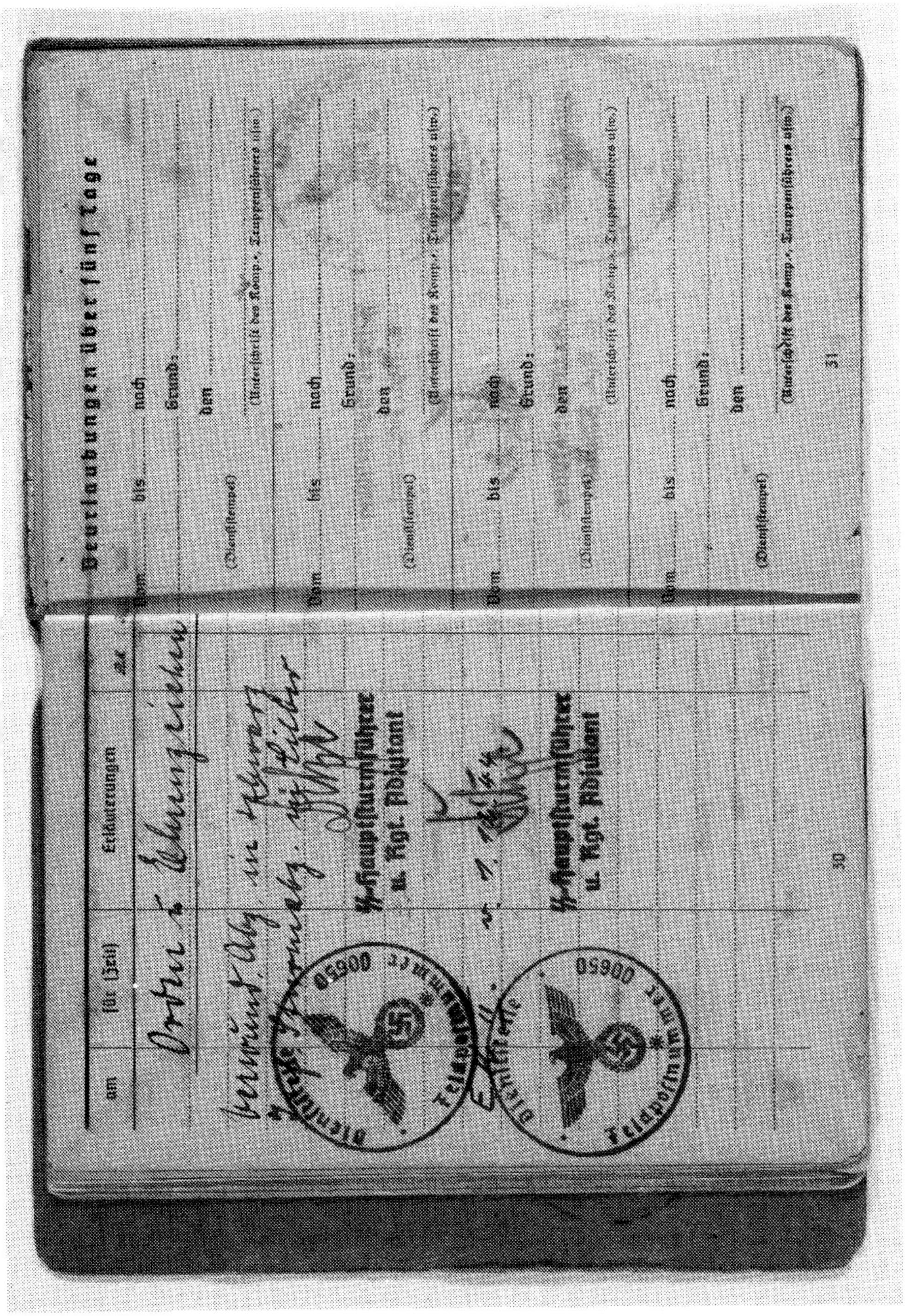
Beurlaubungen über fünf Tage
Erläuterungen
Feldpostnummer 00650
Rgt. Adjutant
Rgt. Adjutant

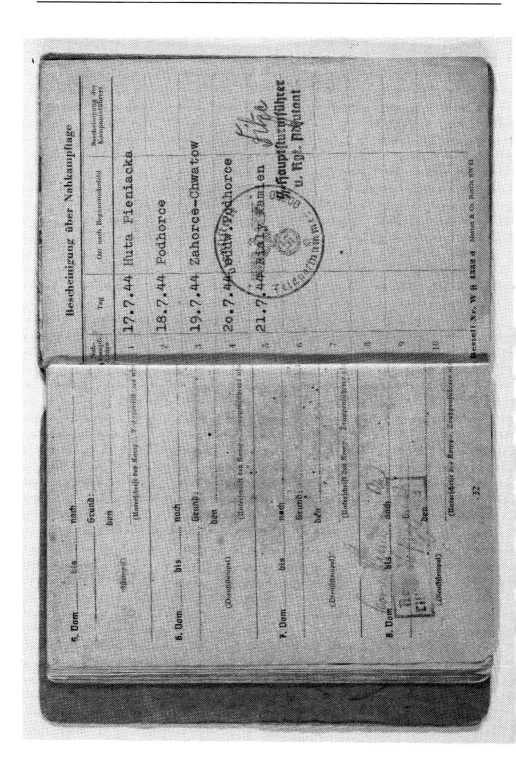

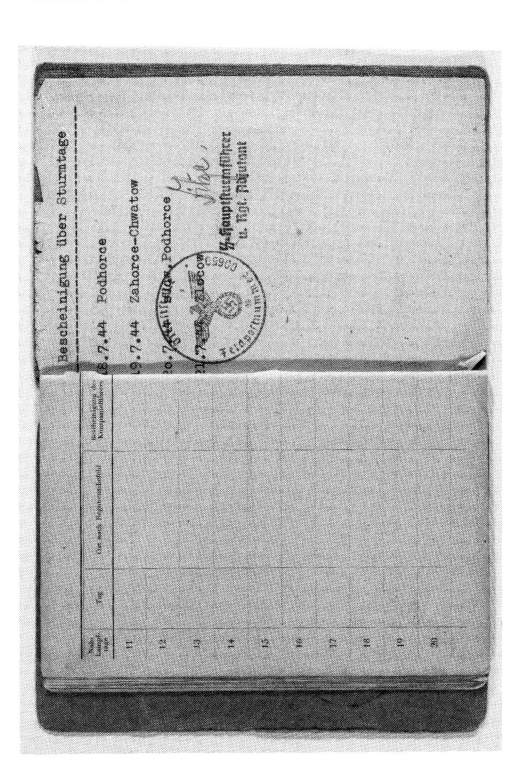

Action in Slovenia and Styria

On 26 January 1945 the SS-FHA ordered the transfer of the *14. Waffen-Grenadier-Division der SS* from Slovakia to Styria.[49] The transfer began ten days later, with three march groups[50] departing in heavy snow. While March Group A, in northwestern Slovakia, headed in the direction of Vienna, March Group B headed south through Bratislava into the Wiener Neustadt area. From there the first group went to Bruck, the second to Hartberg. Finally the two march groups, which were traveling on foot, not by rail, arrived near Graz. The soldiers were supposed to cover between 30 and 40 km per day and were given one day to rest every three days. During the movement the columns were attacked several times by enemy aircraft, after which the troops marched only at night.

On reaching Marburgs on 28 February 1945 the division was placed under the Senior SS and Police Commander Alpenland, *SS-Obergruppenführer und General der Waffen-SS und Polizei* Erwin Rösener[51] for anti-partisan operations. The division occupied quarters in Zellnitz.

SS-Brigadeführer Freitag initially committed the troops to secure the quartering area. With the arrival of about 14,000 soldiers in this area, for the next while the numerically-strong partisan units remained passive.[52] It was thus possible to authorize single vehicles to travel the Marburg – Cilli road, which could be seen as an immediate success.

At the beginning of March 1945 numerous Ukrainian units previously under the Order Police were incorporated into the division. At the same time the division saw its first action under the command of *SS-Obergruppenführer* Rösener. The operation was supposed to destroy numerous partisan units assembled in the area north of Laibach in the area of the Menina Planina and the Boskowetz. After an approach march of, in some cases, more than 100 km, the Ukrainians climbed into the more than 1,500-meter-high mountains, and in the Bratislava – Laufen – Sulzbach area tried to drive partisans toward the other units attached to the Senior SS and Police Commander Alpenland. The three-day operation yielded no noteworthy success. As usual, the partisans escaped into the primeval-forest-like terrain.

When the operation showed no success and partisan activity in the division's own quartering area to the northeast increased, the units were ordered back into the Bacher Mountains.

On 18 March 1945 the division commander ordered a four-day operation to clear the rear area of the nearby front of partisans.[53] Coming from the Bossruck Mountains and moving south across the Drau, the units once again combed the Bacher Mountains. The former *Waffen-Grenadier* Ostap Hladkiwskyj (*8./Waffen-Grenadier-Regiment der SS 29*) recalled:

"In February 1945 we began moving to Slovenia. At first we marched by day and after the bombers attacked us only by night. In Slovenia we occupied quarters in a few small

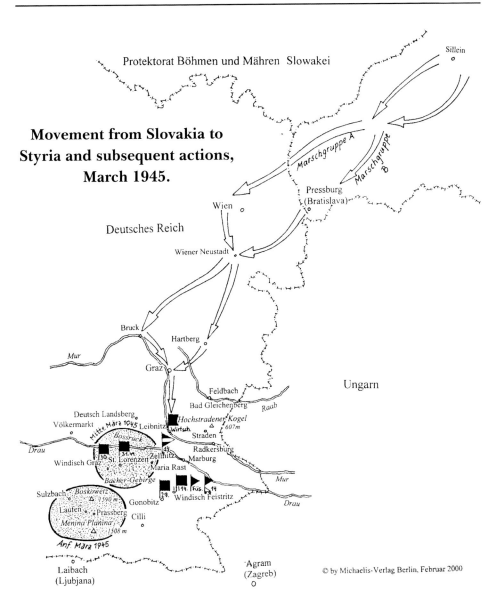

Movement from Slovakia to Styria and subsequent actions, March 1945.

© by Michaelis-Verlag Berlin, Februar 2000

villages and began reconnaissance operations. We were supposed to pursue the Tito partisans by day and night, but normally they eluded us. Only once did we walk into an ambush and had several wounded.

We never had enough sleep and were always hungry. One soldier from our battalion was publicly identified and hung for eating the emergency rations.

While the population in Slovakia was very nice, the Slovenians were just as hostile as the Czechs I met during my training in Bohemia and Moravia."

On 23 March 1945 the OKH ordered the *14. Waffen-Grenadier-Division der SS (ukrainische Nr. 1)* sent to Army Group South.[54] Hitler was made aware of the unit at the evening situation briefing:

Hitler: *"One never knows what's strolling around. Now, to my astonishment, I hear for the first time that a Ukrainian SS division has shown up. I knew absolutely nothing about this Ukrainian SS division."*

Göhler:[55] *"It has existed for a very long time."*

Hitler: *"But it was never mentioned in our conferences. Or do you remember?"*

Göhler: *"No, I don't remember."*

Hitler: *"It may have been brought up to me a long, long time ago, I don't know. How strong is the Ukrainian division?"*

Göhler: *"I will find out."*

Hitler: *"Either the unit is reliable or it isn't reliable. I can't raise units in Germany today because I have no arms. It is nonsense if I go ahead and give arms to a Ukrainian division that is not completely reliable. If that is the case I would rather take its weapons away and raise a German division. I assume that it is excellently armed, probably better armed than most of the German divisions we are raising today."*

Burgdorf:[56] *"It is the same with the Latvian 20th. It has also just been wiped out down there."*[57]

De Maiziére: *"At present the Latvians are fighting up in Courland, and very well at that. The Estonians were down below."*

Burgdorf: *"Yes, the Estonians left immediately. One must also imagine it psychologically. A little much was demanded of them."*

Hitler: *"What are they fighting for anyway? They are away from home."*

Burgdorf: *"If we already have a large number of fainthearted people, it really is impossible to demand much of them."*

Hitler: *"We must now find out exactly which foreign formations are still there. [...] Exactly what is the so-called Galician Division, is it the same as the Ukrainian Division?"*

Borgmann:[58] *"I can't say."*

Hitler: *"There are still stories going around about a Galician Division. Is it the same as the Ukrainian Division? – If it consists of Ruthenes from Austria, there is nothing else to do but immediately take its weapons away. The Austrian Ruthenes were pacifists. They were lambs, but no wolves. They were already miserable in the Austrian Army. It is all a self-deception. Is the Ukrainian Division the same as the so-called Galician Division?"*

Göhler: *"No, the Galician is the 30th, the Ukrainian the 14th. The 30th is resting, in Slovakia I believe."*[59]

Hitler: *"Where did it fight?"*

Göhler: *"The Galician, the 30th, was originally deployed in the Tarnov area and has not been committed since."*

De Maiziére:[60] *"The division took part in the fighting for Lvov as part of the 1st Panzer Army. I believe it was encircled with XIII Corps and only parts of it escaped. As far as I know, it has not been committed since."*

Hitler: *"And it is constantly resting and reequipping? Does it also have weapons?"*

Göhler: *"I will have to find out."*

Hitler: *"We can't allow this game to go on while I am unable to equip other divisions because I have no arms. That is absolutely laughable."*

Göhler: *"The Ukrainian Division has an authorized strength of 11,000 and an actual of 14,000."*

Hitler: *"How is it that actual strength exceeds authorized strength?"*

Göhler: *"They probably have so many Ukrainian recruits above the authorized strength, which they have incorporated into the unit."*

Hitler: *"And the armaments?"*

Göhler: *"They gave much of their arms to the 18th SS."*

Hitler: *"If it is now operational, it appears it again has arms. I will not say that we can't do anything with these foreigners. We can make something of them, but that will take time. If we had them for 6 years or 10 years and the territories were in our own hands like the old monarchy, then of course they would become good soldiers. But if we get them and the territories are somewhere over there – then why should they fight at all? They have access to all the propaganda. I assume that there are also many Germans still there?"*

Göhler: *"Their authorized strength in arms is as follows:[61]*

2,400 pistols	*610 submachine-guns*
9,000 rifles	*70 sniper rifles*
65 K 43 rifles	*434 light machine-guns*
22 flamethrowers	*96 heavy machine-guns*
1 medium anti-tank gun	*11 75-mm anti-tank guns*
9 37-mm anti-aircraft guns	*17 light infantry guns*
3 heavy infantry guns	*37 light field howitzers*
6 heavy field howitzers	*58 trucks*
4 armored troop carriers"	

Hitler: *"That's almost enough to equip two divisions. [...] I must know now what value it has. I would like to speak with the Reichsführer tomorrow. He's in Berlin anyway. There must be a careful check to determine what we can expect of such a unit. If we can expect nothing, then it makes no sense. We cannot allow ourselves the luxury of me having such units."*

Following the discussion between Hitler and Himmler, Army Group South was informed that the transfer of the *14. Waffen-Grenadier-Division der SS (ukrainische Nr.1)* had been cancelled and that orders were to be issued for it to be disarmed. All materiel was to be handed over to the 10th Parachute Division (General Staff *Oberst* von Hoffmann) then being formed.[62]

Interestingly, *SS-Brigadeführer* Freitag, who was usually so negative, drove to the field headquarters of the *Reichsführer-SS* in Salzburg to try to prevent this. The orders were subsequently confirmed and withdrawn several times. Finally, on 28 March 1945 a message came from the field headquarters that the order for the disarming of the *14. Waffen-Grenadier-Division der SS* in favor of the 10th *Luftwaffe* Parachute Division had been rescinded.

The *14. Waffen-Grenadier-Division der SS* was assembled in the Marburg area in preparation for transfer to the 2nd Panzer Army. Battle groups were formed by dividing the heavy weapons among the grenadier regiments, and these initially took up positions in and around Marburg. SS Fusilier Battalion 14 secured the bridge over the Mur near Spielfeld.

Finally, the *14. Waffen-Grenadier-Division der SS* moved north, taking up position behind the boundary between the 2nd Panzer Army and the 6th Army in the role of reserve. At that time enemy troops were massing in the Gleichenberg – Feldbach area in preparation for an assault toward Graz. On Holy Saturday, 31 March 1945, the Red Army breached the Reich Defense Position, which ran along the present-day border between Austria and Hungary. Attached to the 1st Cavalry Corps (2nd Panzer Army), on 1 April the *14. Waffen-Grenadier-Division der SS* received orders to close the gap that had been created between the two armies.

With Soviet tanks from Bad Gleichenberg advancing over the hills between Mühldorf and Feldbach into the Raab Valley and others driving into the same valley from Ferching, with the objective of linking up in Feldbach, at 0630 hours reinforced Waffen-Grenadier Regiments 29 and 30 launched a counterattack. *Waffen-Grenadier-Regiment der SS 31* was initially held back in reserve.

After a few hours the commanding hills in the attack area were in the hands of the Ukrainians. Red Army counterattacks were repulsed in fierce fighting, but when further heavy attacks forced the intervention of the 3rd Cavalry Division, *SS-Brigadeführer* Freitag again lost his nerve. The commanding general of the I Cavalry Corps (*General der Kavallerie* von Harteneck[63]) ordered him to remain in command of his division, however. The fighting was heavy, but most of the positions were held. Ostap Hladkiwskyj (*8./Waffen-Grenadier-Regiment der SS 29*) recalled:

> *"After a long march with our heavy machine-guns and carriages plus the ammunition, we came to a town and dug ourselves in. A few days later we moved to Gleichenberg Castle, but we only stayed there a few hours and then moved again. This time we dug ourselves in on a mountain. The enemy tried to lull us in with propaganda and Ukrainian songs. While the music played all was quiet, but when it stopped we immediately began shooting.*
>
> *One afternoon an artillery observer was able to see the enemy movements clearly. He passed target information to the artillery, but they replied that they could not or must not expend any ammunition.*
>
> *The next morning the enemy began pounding our positions with artillery and mortar fire. Several of our machine-gun positions were hit and many comrades were killed or wounded. Below us we could see several units pulling back. Everything was in flames, horses ran around loose and Red Army troops advanced. Then we received a fire order—we were happy to get rid of our ammunition.*
>
> *When we had used up all the ammunition the enemy came up the mountain. I threw my hand grenades before we withdrew. We gathered near a group of trees. I suddenly found myself with the 4th Company and I immediately dug myself in."*

While the bulk of the division was at the front around Feldbach, SS Pioneer Battalion 14 was still building positions in Marburg, while from Spielfeld SS Fusilier Battalion 14 had been attached to the 23rd Panzer Division (*Generalleutnant* von Radowitz[64]) in the Radkersburg area.[65]

In those days the 14th SS Division's sector of the front ran from south of the east end of Feldbach to and including Gleichenberg (left wing of the 2nd Panzer Army). The three grenadier regiments next to each other at the front were now reinforced through the addition of SS Fusilier Battalion 14 and SS Pioneer Battalion 14, which had been sent to the division to form its reserve.[66] On the division's left was the 5th SS Panzer Division, while on its right first the 3rd and then the 4th Cavalry Division.

On 6-7 April there was heavy fighting for possession of Gleichenberg. The Ukrainians soon lost the Hochstradner Kogel (609 m). This was retaken by the II/Cavalry Regiment 32 (3rd Cavalry Division), which counterattacked via Wilhelmsdorf and Frutten. In the night fighting there were regrettable cases of mistaken identity between Ukrainians, Germans, and Red Army soldiers. A former member of Cavalry Regiment 32 recalled:

Combat in the Reich Defense Position
April/May 1945.

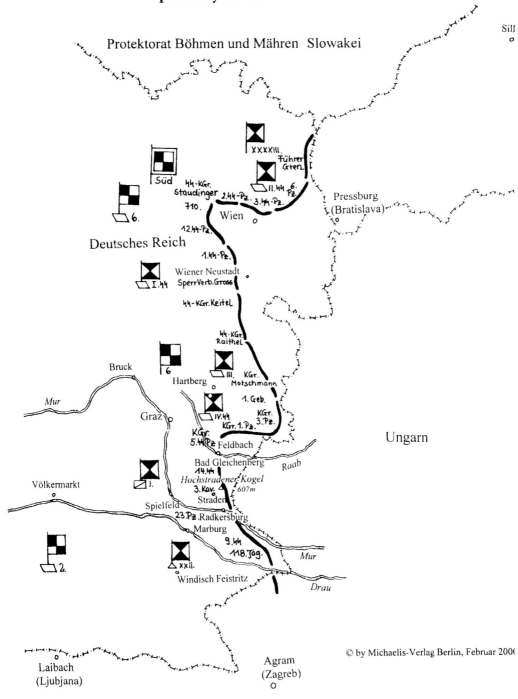

Protektorat Böhmen und Mähren Slowakei

Sill

XXXXIII. Führer Gren.

Süd

ᚼᚼ-KGr. Staudinger
710.

2.ᚼᚼ-Pz. 3.ᚼᚼ-Pz.

II.ᚼᚼ 6.Pz.

6.

Wien

12.ᚼᚼ-Pz.

Pressburg (Bratislava)

Deutsches Reich

1.ᚼᚼ-Pz.

Wiener Neustadt
SperrVerb. Gross

I.ᚼᚼ

ᚼᚼ-KGr. Keitel

ᚼᚼ-KGr. Raithel

Bruck

6

III.

KGr. Motschmann

Hartberg

1. Geb.

Mur

Graz

IV.ᚼᚼ

KGr. 3.Pz.

KGr. 1.Pz.

KGr. 5.ᚼᚼ Pz. Feldbach

Ungarn

Bad Gleichenberg
14.ᚼᚼ

Raab

Völkermarkt

I.

Hochstradener Kogel
3.Kav.   607m
Strader

Spielfeld

23.Pz. Radkersburg

Marburg

9.ᚼᚼ
118.Jäg.

Mur

2.

XXII.

Windisch Feistritz

Drau

Laibach
(Ljubjana)

Agram
(Zagreb)

© by Michaelis-Verlag Berlin, Februar 200(

"The fighting went on until dawn. Afterwards the Ukrainians broke into tears when they discovered that they had wounded at least five of our soldiers… We drove the Russians down the Kogel to the east. There two self-propelled anti-aircraft guns were able to join the fighting. They fired into the fleeing Russians… A frightful massacre! On 8 April came the order to attack toward St. Anna. It wasn't until noon that the artillery showed up. The preparatory fire was pitiful because of a shortage of ammunition… We pulled back toward the Kogel and came under heavy enemy mortar fire in the forest there. The day had cost the battalion three killed and ten wounded.

The Ukrainians took over with trembling hearts and raced back up the entire Kogel and we went to Haag in reserve. No sooner had we got something to eat when the Ukrainians took off again and the Russians regained the mountain. We were forced to attack once again. I came upon a Ukrainian Waffen-Untersturmführer. Enraged, I screamed at him, whereupon he put his pistol to his head and threatened to pull the trigger. His soldiers around him chanted in chorus `Swaboda, Swaboda' (freedom). I calmed them down with a few words like 'Pomalu' and 'Pakoy' (quiet). A few days later the Waffen-Untersturmführer was killed near Stallhans during a joint counterattack…

On 10 April, near Bad Gleichenberg in the Ukrainians' sector, we had to make an attack against some Russians who had broken through. We literally went up one side of the mountain and down the other and there was shooting in all directions. The heavy weapons were unable to support us. For several hours there was heavy fighting for possession of the small station in Trautmannsdorf. Nearby was the mountain castle of Gleichenberg. It was heavily fired on and destroyed…"

Gleichenberg Castle belonged to the family of Count Stubenberg. The countess recalled:

"Gleichenberg Castle was the property of the Trautmannsdorf family, of which my mother was a member. She transferred ownership to me, however I spent my youth at our estate in Bohemia. I spent the Second World War at my husband's home. Not until 1946 did I leave Geiersberg and move to Gleichenberg. The beautiful castle was in ruins, as the final battles had been fought there. We found everything plundered and fallen down.

I know that artillery on the Kogel had bombarded the castle. I often heard that there had been Ukrainian soldiers in the castle. There were also many young soldiers buried in the forest. They still had their identity discs around their necks. I saw that for myself when the gravedigger exhumed them in 1947. The entire forest around our house was also sewn with anti-tank mines, which were later removed."

On 6 April 1945 the *Wehrmacht* communiqué declared:

"On the Upper Raab, counterattacks by our forces retook Feldbach and Fehring and cleared the enemy from other areas."

On 8 April 1945 a mass was held in the church in Paldau according to the Slavic rite. A choir from the division also sang. A female resident recalled:

"A local priest, who happened to be there, took part and gave the mass in Ukrainian. A wonderful-sounding men's choir helped celebrate the mass by singing the old songs of the Easter Liturgy. Slavic rite services were also held on the Salzkogel."

On 8 April 1945 the *Wehrmacht* High Command announced:

"In the German-Hungarian border region, after days of heavy offensive and defensive fighting units of the army and the Waffen-SS have halted the enemy advance in the direction of Graz and restored the temporarily-breached front."

In mid-April the division was attached to the 6th Army (*General der Panzertruppen* Balck[67]). There the Ukrainians were committed as part of the IV SS Panzer Corps (*SS-Obergruppenführer* Gille[68]). The division's sector from Feldbach to Gleichenberg was extended to the northern limits of the town of Feldbach (right wing of the 6th Army).

On 15 April 1945, after several days of quiet, the Red Army resumed the offensive with the objective of taking Gleichenberg. Counterattacking with small arms, the Ukrainians were able to retake the hills previously occupied by the Red Army. Afterwards the front in this sector became quiet and remained so until the end of the war.

When English troops moved into the Klagenfurt area at the beginning of May 1945, the unit, now calling itself the 1st Division of the Ukrainian National Army,[69] made contact in hope of being taken prisoner by the Western Allies. With the understanding of the English the Ukrainian units were to march to the 14th SS Waffen-Grenadier Training and Replacement Regiment in the area around Völkermarkt, and if necessary offer resistance against Tito partisans.

There was also an order from the ranking IV SS Panzer Corps, according to which the division was supposed to head north toward the Radstädter Tauer. The growing signs of disintegration—for example, officers abandoning their units to avoid being taken prisoner—made it difficult to keep order in the final days.

While the soldiers moved out in long columns, in Paldau the pioneer battalion blew up a large department store to block the Feldbach - St. Stefan road to the Red Army.

Marching along the Mur, on 10 May 1945 the division reached Tamsweg. From there elements reached Radstadt with IV Panzer Corps and others, Spittal, and from there a POW camp in Rimini. The Ukrainians were fortunate that most of them came from Galicia (Poland), and were thus not handed over to the Soviet Union. After the war some went to Canada, England, or Australia, while others remained in Austria and Germany.

Former *Waffen-Grenadier* B.S. (14th SS Waffen-Grenadier Training and Replacement Regiment) wrote:

"Luckily we also had no contact with the enemy in Styria. Our company was extremely disciplined and morale was excellent. The German surrender didn't surprise us, we expected it. Only the timing was unknown to us. I then left the unit and went to Bavaria to avoid becoming a prisoner of war."

SS-Unterscharführer Hümmer (14th SS Medical Battalion) recalled:

"In January-February 1945 we marched on foot via the Lesser Carpathians, Vienna, Semmering, Styria to Marburg/Drau in the Bacher Mountains. The final action took place in the Radkersburg area, where we set up our main dressing station. The entire way I and several men assigned to me were responsible for riding ahead on bicycles and finding quarters for our medical battalion. One of my best friends was SS-Unterscharführer Horst Hersener, who came from the former German colony of Southwest Africa. Horst stayed behind in Sillein as cleanup detachment and followed later. The entire division was supposed to surrender to the Russians at Lake Millstadt in Carinthia, but after the surrender we broke up behind Graz and everyone was free to do what he thought right. I went over the mountains to Salzburg, then to Munich. I was taken prisoner near Regensburg on 29 May 1945."

Former *SS-Unterscharführer* Erich Rommel (H.Q./*Waffen-Grenadier-Regiment der SS 29*) described the final weeks of the war:

"In November 1944 I rejoined Waffen-Grenadier-Regiment der SS 29 near Sillein (Kys. Nowe Mesto), where I received the Iron Cross, Second Class. In February 1945 our division marched in snow and ice through Slovakia and Austria to Slovenia for operations against partisans.

At the beginning of April 1945 there was action in the Bad Gleichenberg area, Radkersburg (Styria) on the border between Slovenia and Hungary. On about 12 May 1945 the bulk of the division was captured by the English. In summer 1945 the order was given to release all Ukrainians. The former division was distributed in the Radstadt – Flachau area. We Germans worked day and night to fill out the release papers, which were signed by the English. I also took part. We were told that all the Ukrainians would be released in the Munich area. Then in 1947 I was also released from the Dachau camp."

Former *SS-Obersturmführer* Bernhard Dornbusch wrote:

"Two days before the end of the war I was given a special mission by SS-Brigadeführer Freitag. I was supposed to search for the division's Ic, SS-Hauptsturmführer Niermann, who had already fled. It was suspected that he and his wife, whom he had met in the Marburg area, had gone to Graz. The police refused to help with the planned search, and when we approached Gestapo post commanders and told them that SS officers were running away, they also ran away from us.

The next day I learned from the commander of the SS Medical Academy Graz, who was returning from district headquarters, that the Russians were expected in the afternoon. I subsequently made my way to the field replacement battalion in Hitzendorf and learned that the division was going to withdraw across the Pack to Carinthia. On the way there I heard about the surrender in an outdoor cafe in Köflach.

As we were released as German core personnel of the 14. Waffen-Grenadier-Division der SS, I stayed by the Pack for a few days and was captured there. At first I was locked up in the indoor riding arena of the Lipizzaner stud farm in Piber; my captivity lasted until 15 March 1948. Then I was interned for three years."

Thus ended the story of the SS Volunteer Division Galicia. In addition to the division commander, who was unsuited to command such a unit, a considerable number of the core personnel were former members of the Order Police and *Waffen-SS* who had been released by their units for reasons of unsuitability. This could have been because of age or lack of military ability.

Because of the fact many German soldiers saw assignment to a foreign formation as a demotion, most of the core personnel also lacked the necessary motivation. As a unit is, as a rule, only as good as its officers, this state of affairs had a negative effect on the division's operational capabilities.

Some of the Ukrainian volunteers joined the division because of their desire for national sovereignty, but different circumstances soon caused them to lose their drive. Like many others they could be enthused quickly, but disillusionment soon set in. The former Austrian Hitler dismissed the Galician Ukrainians as "*Lambs [...], [who were] miserable in the Austrian Army.*"

And so the only advantage, if any, that Germany gained from the formation and employment of the *14. Waffen-Grenadier-Division der SS (ukrainische Nr. 1)* was propagandistic.

Bernhard Dornbusch

The grave of
SS-Brigadeführer Freitag
in St. Andrä, near Tamsweg.

The author with a Ukrainian veteran at a memorial in Styria erected in 1976.

Memorial to the soldiers killed in Styria.

Ukrainian veterans visit the scene of the Brody fighting, 1999.

БРАТСТВО КОЛ. ВОЯКІВ ПЕРШОЇ УКРАЇНСЬКОЇ ДИВІЗІЇ (1. УД УНА)
КРАЙОВА УПРАВА В НІМЕЧЧИНІ

BRUDERSCHAFT EHEM. SOLDATEN DER 1. UKRAINISCHEN DIVISION e. V.

DACHAUER STR. 9/2, 8000 MÜNCHEN 2

München, den 24.09.1998

Michaelis - Verlag
Postfach 520 341
12593 Berlin
Tel./Fax.Nr. 030-56495 615

Sehr geehrter Herr Michaelis !

Im Namen unserer Bruderschaft bedanke ich mich herzlich
für Ihre Arbeit über die 14. SS-Divison "Galizien"(1.Ukra-
inische).

Sie zeichnet sich durch die exakte und objektive Schil-
derung der Ereignisse aus.

Ihr Werk ist eine wichtige Dokumentation zur Geschichte
der fremdenvölkirschen Divisionen der deutschen Wahrmacht
im II. Weltkrieg.

Ich werde Ihre Arbeit jedem Liebhaber der militärischen
Literatur empfehlen.

Mit besten Wünschen
und kameradschaftlichen Grüßen

Bohdan Szarko
Obmann

Schreiben der Truppenkameradschaft.

Letter to the author from the veterans group.

Appendices

Appendix 1

The Ukraine
in the Mirror
of the Twentieth Century

The history of the Ukraine goes back to the 9th Century even before Austrian rule. At that time the present-day north and west Ukraine formed the core of the Kiev Empire, which was destroyed by the Mongols in 1240. In 1320 the region went to Lithuania and in 1569 with it to Poland. In 1654 the country was taken over by the Moscow Tsars, who felt they were linked by orthodoxy. The southern area, still a border region (Ukraina) extended itself further toward the Crimea. In 1772 the West Ukraine (first called Galicia) fell to Austria, followed two years later by Bukovina (Buchenland). This favored closer ties with Rome, to which the West-Ukrainian church had aligned itself in 1546. From that time there was the Orthodox Church in Kiev and the Greek-Catholic in Lvov. Both followed the Slavic rite. The East Ukraine and Wolhynia remained part of the Russian empire.

In August 1914 Russian troops entered Austrian Galicia and conquered the city of Lvov (Lemberg). The Tsarist forces suppressed all national movements with the intention of Russifying the entire Ukrainian population of Galicia and the Carpathian Ukraine. When they were driven out of the region by Austrian and German forces in 1915, they deported a large number of Ukrainians. At the same time the desire arose in nationalist Ukrainian circles to unite Eastern Galicia with the other Ukrainian provinces into their own state.

On 17 December 1917, after the ceasefire with Germany and Austria, Lenin declared the Ukraine a sovereign and independent nation. In spite of this Russian troops entered the country one week later. On 8 February 1918 the Ukrainian government was forced to leave Kiev and move to Zhitomir. It turned to Germany and Austria-Hungary, which recognized the Ukraine as an independent nation and provided its army with weapons with which to fight bolshevism. In return the Ukraine was to deliver one million tons of wheat. After the Treaty of Brest-Litovsk was signed on 9 February 1918, German and Austrian troops supported the Ukrainian Army and occupied the East Ukraine until the end of the First World War.

On 1 November 1918 Galicia, the Bukovina and the Carpathian Ukraine formed the West Ukrainian National Republic, which on 3 January 1919 joined the Ukrainian National Republic. At the same time, in Moscow Stalin set up a Ukrainian Soviet government, which in 1920 won the political struggle against the nationalists and took over the reigns of government. The Peace of Riga resulted in the country being divided once more: Galicia became Polish70, the Carpathian Ukraine Czech and the Bukovina was promised to Rumania.

In 1922 the East Ukraine became part of the Soviet Union. The East-Ukrainian population suffered terribly as a result: an artificially-induced famine killed millions in 1932-33. Stalin's subjugation led to a deep hatred of Russia and caused the old desire for an autonomous Ukraine to steadily grow.

On 23 August 1939 Germany and the Soviet Union signed a friendship pact. A few weeks later—at the end of the campaign in Poland—on 22 September 1939 the Red Army marched into Lvov. One moth later a staged communist national assembly requested that Galicia be incorporated into the Ukrainian Soviet Republic. After fighting with Ukrainian rebels71, Hungarian troops marched into the Carpathian Ukraine, which until 1939 had been part of Czechoslovakia and then occupied by Poland.

"Operation Barbarossa" began on 22 June 1941. During the rapid retreat by the Red Army, the NKVD shot thousands of political opponents, causing hatred of Stalin and the USSR to reach a new height.

As a western-oriented country, the Ukraine had always hoped for help from Germany or Austria in its struggle against Sovietization, and as National-Socialist Germany was the only legitimate anti-Soviet power at that time, politicians tried to reach a consensus with Hitler. On 23 June 1941 the Organization of Ukrainian Nationalists (OUN) passed a memorandum to the German government which offered Ukrainian assistance in the struggle against bolshevism on the condition of national sovereignty. One week later the Ukraine declared its independence.

Hitler had no interest in an autonomous Ukrainian state, however, instead he viewed the country as a vital source of raw materials. In response to the declaration of independence, leading personalities (such as Bandera[72], Melnyk and Dr. Rebet[73]) were arrested and placed in concentration camps.

In August 1941 part of the West Ukraine, which belonged to Austria in the time of the Imperial Monarchy, was attached to the General Government (General Governor Frank74) in 1939, as the District of Galicia.75 This was only a part, however, of the original Galicia, which geographically extended to Cracow. Previously the western part of Galicia had already formed the District of Cracow. Of interest is the fact that the inhabitants were actually Ukrainians who, though they were of the Catholic faith, principally felt and spoke as Ukrainians. The rest of the Ukraine, which was Orthodox, was combined into the Reich Commissariat Ukraine under Gauleiter Erich Koch76. These measures very quickly reversed the sympathy previously felt toward Germany.

A different policy was pursued by the governor of the District of Galicia, *SS-Brigadeführer* Dr. Otto Wächter, who—probably as a result of his Austrian background—wanted to allow the West Ukrainians as much freedom and economic wellbeing as possible.

In 1941 the Ukrainian population greeted the German forces as liberators and allies. Disillusionment was not long in coming...

SS-Brigadeführer Dr. Wächter visits young Ukrainian *Luftwaffe* auxiliaries.

Appendix 2
Chronology

28/04/43 – 02/44	Formation at the SS training camp in Heidelager
16/02/44 – 20/03/44	SS Battle Group Beyersdorff in action against partisans in the Zamosc area
03/44 – 25/06/44	Formation continues at the SS training camp in Neuhammer
25/06/44 – 14/07/44	Attached to the XIII Army Corps
15/07/44 – 24/07/44	Fighting and breakout from the Brody Pocket
08/44 – 27/09/44	Reformation at the SS training camp in Neuhammer
07/44 – 04/11/44	1,000 Ukrainian soldiers see action with the 5. *SS-Panzer-Division Wiking*
28/09/44 – 18/10/44	SS Battle Group Wildner in action against partisans in Slovakia
17/10/44 – 15/11/44	SS Battle Group Wittenmeyer and one other in action against partisans in Slovakia
07/10/44 – 05/02/45	Reformation continues in Slovakia
28/02/45 – 28/03/45	Anti-partisan operations in Slovenia
30/03/45 – 09/05/45	Action with I Cavalry Corps and IV SS Panzer Corps in the Feldbach area

Appendix 3

Renaming as the 1st Division of the Ukrainian National Army

Beginning in mid-1944 there was a noticeable shift in Germany's eastern policy. In July 1944 *SS-Sturmbannführer* Dr. Arlt, who had studied East European history and headed the Nationalities Department in the General Government, was placed in charge of the new Volunteer Coordination Center East in the *SS Hauptamt* (Head Office). Head of the Ukraine Subsection was *SS-Obersturmbannführer* Ludwig Wolff, who had been removed as district leader in Lodz (Litzmannstadt) on account of his opposition to German actions there. In their combined search for a national leader personality, who was to give the volunteer movement fresh impetus, they tried to recruit the later Ukrainian General Schandruk, born in Wolhynia in 1889. He had commanded a Polish regiment in 1939 and had been released from a German POW camp in 1940. Although he rejected the rank of an *SS-Gruppenführer*, Schandruk agreed under certain conditions.

With the steady Allied advance and the loss of the occupied areas in the Soviet Union, Hitler was now willing to make concessions to the various eastern countries desiring autonomy. Ultimately he even approved the formation of a Ukrainian National Committee proposed by Alfred Rosenberg. Ukrainian politicians locked up in German concentration camps in 1941 were set free (Bandera on 25 September 1944, Melnyk on 17 October 1944).

On 15 November 1944 in Prague, Vlasov78 proclaimed the Committee to Liberate the Peoples of Russia. The Ukrainians were critical of this proclamation—they feared a renewed Russian patronage by Vlasov and tried to retain their slowly-achieved sovereignty.79

Without the likelihood of Germany being able to keep its promises, however, the Ukrainians lacked the morale of 1941. Thus the renaming of the *14. Waffen-Grenadier-Division der SS* from **Galician No. 1** to **Ukrainian No. 1** on 15 January 1945 no longer had any effect.80

When General Schandruk was named Commander-in-Chief of the Armed Forces of the Ukrainian National Committee in April 1945, the *14. Waffen-Grenadier-Division der SS (ukrainische Nr. 1)* received the designation **1st Division of the Ukrainian National Army**. As well the Ukrainian national anthem was introduced as the division song, a new oath was sworn to the Ukraine and Ukrainian became the language of command and orders.

A 2nd Division was also in the process of being established under the command of Colonel Diatshenko.81 At the end of April 1945 General Schandruk, as commander of all Ukrainian units, visited the division and brought with him cap cockades authorized by Hitler as well as collar patches bearing the trident for the Ukrainian volunteers. Ostap Hladkiwskyj recalled:

"In the end we were even designated the Ukrainian National Army. We had to lay down our arms and after this symbolic gesture we swore a new oath to the Ukraine. Armed again, we moved back into the front line."

The renaming in spring 1945 from Galician to Ukrainian division and to the 1st Division of the Ukrainian National Army in April of that year had symbolic value only.

Appendix 4

Military Postal Numbers and Holders of Command Positions

Division Headquarters	F.P.Nr. 15 000	SS-Brigadeführer Walter Schimana
		SS-Brigadeführer Fritz Freitag
Adjutant		SS-Sturmbannführer Erich Finder
Ia		SS-Hauptsturmführer Otto Behrendt
		SS-Sturmbannführer Wolf-Dietrich Heike
1st Staff Officer		SS-Obersturmführer Michel
Ib		SS-Hauptsturmführer Herbert Schaaf
2nd Staff Officer		SS-Obersturmführer Ruwenon
Ic		SS-Obersturmführer Günther Nußbach
		SS-Hauptsturmführer Fritz Niermann
3rd Staff Officer		SS-Obersturmführer Schenker
IIa		SS-Obersturmführer Erich Finder
III		SS-Hauptsturmführer Gerhard Herrmann
		SS-Sturmbannführer Ziegler
IVa		SS-Sturmbannführer Otto Sulzbach
		SS-Sturmbannführer Armin Engel
IVb		SS-Obersturmbannführer Dr. Max Specht
		SS-Sturmbannführer Dr. Friedrich-Wilhelm Lüdke
		SS-Sturmbannführer Dr. Georg Coldewey
Division Pharmacist		SS-Hauptsturmführer Werner Beneke
IVc		SS-Sturmbannführer Dr. Oskar Knopp
		SS-Sturmbannführer Dr. Thomas Andresen
Division Engineer		SS-Sturmbannführer Hans Schrader
Commander/Headquarters		SS-Obersturmführer Ernst Gebhardt

Waffen-Grenadier-Regiment der SS 29 (ukrainische Nr. 1)

Headquarters	F.P.Nr. 00 650	SS-Standartenführer Fritz Dern
Adjutant		SS-Hauptsturmführer Ditze
Regimental Medical Officer		SS-Untersturmführer Dr.Kowalski
I Batallion	F.P.Nr. 03 368	SS-Hauptsturmführer Heinz Kurzbach
		SS-Hauptsturmführer Otto Blankenhorn
II Batallion	F.P.Nr. 07 226	SS-Hauptsturmführer Wilhelm Allerkamp
		SS-Hauptsturmführer Hans Sulzinger
III Battalion	F.P.Nr. 19 223	SS-Obersturmbannführer Karl Wildner
13th Company	F.P.Nr. 18 410	
14th Company	F.P.Nr. 04 569	

Waffen-Grenadier-Regiment der SS 30 (ukrainische Nr. 2)

Headquarters	F.P.Nr. 05 330	SS-Obersturmbannführer Hans-Boto Forstreuter
		SS-Standartenführer Fritz Dern
Adjutant		SS-Hauptsturmführer Kurkowsky
I Battalion	F.P.Nr. 09 084	SS-Hauptsturmführer Siegfried Klocker
II Battalion	F.P.Nr. 10 227	SS-Hauptsturmführer Friedrich Wittenmeyer
III Battalion	F.P.Nr. 23 374	SS-Hauptsturmführer Albert Zerwin
13th Company	F.P.Nr. 18 410	
14th Company	F.P.Nr. 13 283	

Waffen-Grenadier-Regiment der SS 31 (ukrainische Nr. 3)

Headquarters	F.P.Nr. 11 088	SS-Obersturmbannführer Paul Herms
		SS-Standartenführer Rudolf Pannier82
Adjutant		SS-Hauptsturmführer Günter Weiß
Regimental Chaplain		Waffen-Untersturmführer Lewinsky
I Battalion	F.P.Nr. 19 265	SS- Sturmbannaführer Heinz Kurzbach
II Battalion	F.P.Nr. 16 138	SS-Sturmbannführer Elmar Scholtz
III Battalion	F.P.Nr. 28 714	SS- Sturmbannführer Podlesch
13th Company	F.P.Nr. 14 295	
14th Company	F.P.Nr. 17 082	

Waffen-Artillerie-Regiment der SS 14 (ukrainische Nr. 1)

Headquarters	F.P.Nr. 02 002	SS-Obersturmbannführer Friedrich Beyersdorff
Adjutant		SS-Obersturmführer Helmut Horstmann
I Battalion	F.P.Nr. 21 985	SS-Hauptsturmführer Kurt Gläss
II Battalion	F.P.Nr. 15 107	SS-Sturmbannführer Alfred Schützendörfer
		SS-Hauptsturmführer Emil Schlesinger
III Battalion	F.P.Nr. 20 213	SS-Hauptsturmführer Günther Sparsam
IV Battalion	F.P.Nr. 25 614	SS-Sturmbannführer Otto Beissel

SS-Nachschubtruppen 14 (14th SS Supply Unit)

Headquarters	F.P.Nr. 31 283	SS-Obersturmbannführer Franz Magill
Adjutant		SS-Sturmbannführer Haase
1st Motor Transport Company	F.P.Nr. 23 908	
2nd Motor Transport Company	F.P.Nr. 27 423	
1st/2nd Bicycle Company	F.P.Nr. 26 918	
Supply Company	F.P.Nr. 22 510	
Workshop Company	F.P.Nr. 28 612	SS-Hauptsturmführer Martiniuk

SS-Wirtschaftsbataillon 14

Headquarters	F.P.Nr. 06 771	SS-Obersturmbannführer Sulzbach
Adjutant		SS-Obersturmführer Mayer
Bakery Company	F.P.Nr. 31 935	
Butcher Company	F.P.Nr. 25 107	
Supply Office	F.P.Nr. 19 432	
Veterinary Company	F.P.Nr. 27 592	SS-Hauptsturmführer Dr. Andresen
SS Field Post Office	F.P.Nr. 29 400	SS-Obersturmführer Hielscher

SS-Sanitäts-Abteilung 14 (14th SS Medical Battalion)

Headquarters	F.P.Nr. 12 102	SS-Sturmbannführer Dr. Max Specht
Adjutant		SS-Obersturmführer Dr. Günther
Administrative Officer		SS-Obersturmführer Dirksheide
Staff Scharführer		SS-Oberscharführer Karl Friedrich
1st Company	F.P.Nr. 22 317	SS-Sturmbannführer Dr. Schmitt
2nd Company	F.P.Nr. 18 480	SS-Hauptsturmführer Dr. Stridde
1st Ambulance Platoon	F.P.Nr. 24 661	
2nd Ambulance Platoon	F.P.Nr. 30 109	
Field Hospital	F.P.Nr. 44 741	SS-Sturmbannführer Dr. Schmitt

Waffen-Grenadier-Ausbildugs- und Ersatz-Regiment der SS 14
14th SS Waffen Grenadier Training and Replacement Regiment

Headquarters	F.P.Nr. 39 336	SS-Standartenführer Mathias Huber
		SS-Obersturmbannführer Carl Marcks
Adjutant		SS-Hauptsturmführer Roggenkamp
I Battalion	F.P.Nr. 67 249	SS-Hauptsturmführer Hartung
II Battalion	F.P.Nr. 37 682	SS-Hauptsturmführer Pöhle
III Battalion	F.P.Nr. 64 425	SS-Sturmbannführer Schramm

SS-Feldersatz-Bataillon 14 (14th SS Field Replacement Battalion)

	F.P.Nr. 28 966	SS-Sturmbannführer Joannes Kleinow
Adjutant		SS-Untersturmführer Reichenbach

SS-Fusilier-Bataillon 14

	F.P.Nr. 01 461	SS-Sturmbannführer Josef Syr
		SS-Obersturmbannführer Karl Bristot
Adjutant		SS-Obersturmführer Schmitten

SS-Panzerjäger-Abteilung 14 (14th SS Anti-Tank Battalion)

	F.P.Nr. 30 904	SS-Sturmbannführer Herbert Kaschner
Adjutant		SS-Untersturmführer Kellner

SS-Pionier-Bataillon 14

	F.P.Nr. 29 826	SS-Sturmbannführer Josef Remberger
Adjutant		SS-Untersturmführer Horst Glöckner

SS-Nachrichten-Abteilung 14 (14th SS Signals Battalion)

	F.P.Nr. 24 047	SS-Hauptsturmführer Wolfgang Wuttig
		SS-Sturmbannführer Werner Heinz
Adjutant		SS-Untersturmführer Kaufmann

Appendix 5

Waffen-SS/Wehrmacht Ranks 1944

SS-Grenadier	Waffen-Grenadier[84]	Grenadier
SS-Sturmmann	Waffen-Sturmmann	Gefreiter
SS-Rottenführer	Waffen-Rottenführer	Obergefreiter
SS-Unterscharführer	Waffen-SS-Unterscharrführer	Unteroffizier
SS-Scharführer	Waffen-Scharführer	Unterfeldwebel
SS-Oberscharführer	Waffen-Oberscharführer	Feldwebel
SS-Hauptscharführer	Waffen-Hauptscharführer	Oberfeldwebel
SS-Untersturmführer	Waffen-Untersturmführer	Leutnant
SS-Obersturmführer	Waffen-Obersturmführer	Oberleutnant
SS-Hauptsturmführer	Waffen-Hauptsturmführer	Hauptmann
SS-Sturmbannführer	Waffen-Sturmbannführer	Major
SS-Obersturmbannführer	Waffen-Obersturmbannführer	Oberstleutnant
SS-Standartenführer	Waffen-Standartenführer	Oberst
SS-Oberführer	Waffen-Oberführer	no comparable rank
SS-Brigadeführer	Waffen-Brigadeführer	Generalmajor
SS-Gruppenführer	Waffen-Gruppenführer	Generalleutnant
SS-Obergruppenführer	Waffen-Obergruppenführer	General
SS-Oberstgruppenführer	Waffen-Oberstgruppenführer	Generaloberst

Endnotes

[1] On 1 August 1941 the Commanding General of Security Forces and the commander of Army Group Area South, *Generalleutnant* Karl von Roques, handed over part of the West Ukraine, under occupation since 22 June 1941, to *Reichminister* Dr. Frank, General-Governor of Poland. It became the fifth district (Galicia) with an area of 47,100 km^2 and increased the population by about 4.7 million to approximately 18 million people. Lvov, with about 320,000 inhabitants, became the district capital. Of particular economic importance was agriculture, for the soil was very rich. The district helped ease the burden on the General Government's agricultural budget, for just as in the Lublin District it was possible to produce more than required to feed the local population. The district also produced oil and natural gas, and there was a significant forestry and lumber industry (approx. 25% of the land surface was wooded). Because of two years of Soviet rule and the hardships created by the war, however, there was widespread poverty in Galicia, which was populated by about 1 million Poles and 3.5 million Ukrainians.

[2] Otto Gustav Wächter was born in Vienna on 8 July 1901 and attended school for 12 years. He then began studying law in Vienna, graduating with a doctorate in 1924. Dr. Wächter had already joined the NSDAP the year before. After practicing law in Vienna for seven years, in 1932 he opened his own law practice in the city of his birth and also joined local *SS-Standarte 11*. In July 1924 Wächter was one of the leading figures in the unsuccessful putsch in Austria, in which Chancellor Dollfuß was murdered. On 28 July he moved to Germany and was granted citizenship there in 1935. On 3 October of that year he was promoted to *SS-Untersturmführer*.

Wächter received basic military training in an army replacement battalion in Freising from 17 March to 29 July 1936, and was released with the rank of *Gefreiter (ROA)*. From 10 September 1936 to 15 February 1937 he served in the SD with the rank of *SS-Obersturmbannführer*. With the incorporation of Austria into the German Reich, in March 1938 Wächter returned to his native land and was named by *Reichstatthalter* Dr. Seyß-Inquart to the post of State Secretary for Internal Administration. As an *SS-Standartenführer*, on 1 June 1938 he was sent to the *SS-Oberabschnitt Donau*. On 9 November 1938 he was promoted to *SS-Oberführer* and one year later to *SS-Brigadeführer*.

Following creation of the Cracow District in the newly-created General Government he was appointed governor. In this capacity he took part in the so-called Resettlement Conference in Berlin on 30 January 1940. In August 1941 West-Ukrainian territories were added to the General Government, and he took over these. As district governor of Galicia, on 16 May 1944 Dr. Wächter was given the rank of *SS-Gruppenführer*, which on 24 August was followed by the addition of "*Generalleutnant der Polizei*." On 1 December 1944 he was assigned to the personal staff of the *Reichsführer-SS* and was supposed to function in the liaison role in the combined German and Ukrainian struggle against Stalin. At the end of the war he was with members of the 1st Division of the Ukrainian National Army, and these concealed his identity in the Rimini POW camp. He stayed in Italy and finally lived in a religious faculty in Rome. It is to be assumed that the Catholic Church knew to whom it was providing shelter. On 14 July 1949 Dr. Wächter died at the age of 50 in the Catholic Holy Ghost Hospital in Castelgandolfo.

[3] Gottlob Berger was born in Gerstetten on 16 July 1896. He served as a volunteer in the First World War and his last post was *Leutnant* Adjutant of III./I.R. 476. He was demobilized on 5 February 1920. Two years later, while working as a seminary teacher, Berger joined the Nazi Party. Active in the SA since 1930, on 30 January 1936 he was taken into the SS with the rank of *SS-Oberführer*. On 20 April 1939, with the rank of *SS-Brigadeführer*, he took over the *SS-Ergänzungsamt*. After two years he became head of the *SS-Hauptamt* with the rank of *SS-Gruppenführer*. Promotion to *SS-Obergruppenführer und General der Waffen-SS* followed on 21 June 1943. In addition to functioning as head of the SS-FHA, he was also State Secretary

in the Reich Ministry for the Occupied Eastern Territories (Rosenberg). During the attempt to put down the Slovakian National Uprising in 1944, Berger showed himself to be unfit for the task and was relieved after a few days. For his efforts to expand the *Waffen-SS*, on 15 November 1944 he was awarded the Knight's Cross of the War Merit Cross with Swords. He died in his home town on 5 January 1975.

[4] This later became the *4. SS-Polizei-Panzergrenadier-Division*.

[5] Kurt Daluege was born in Kreuzberg (Upper Silesia) on 15 September 1897. He joined the military as a volunteer in 1916, and after the First World War took part in various military actions by the *Freikorps*. Daluege subsequently studied at the Berlin Technical School and graduated with a Degree in Construction and Civil Engineering. On 12 March 1926 he was accepted into the NSDAP with membership number 31 981. He founded the SA in northern Germany and was made deputy *Gauleiter* in Berlin. From 1927 Daluege worked as a street cleaner in Berlin. In July 1930 he transferred to the SS (No. 1 119), and on 1 March 1931 was named commander of *SS Abschnitt III Berlin*. On 1 July of that year he was promoted to *SS-Gruppenführer* and made commander of *SS-Gruppe-Ost*.

Daluege had been a member of the legislature in Prussia since 1932, and then Prussian Minister of the Interior Göring appointed him Special State Secretary. On 13 September 1933 Daluege was given the rank of *Generalmajor der Landespolizei* and named Commander of Police in Prussia. Promoted to *SS-Obergruppenführer* on 9 September 1934, on 20 April 1935 the suffix *Generalleutnant der Landespolizei* was added to his rank. Named *General der Polizei* on 17 June 1936, on 26 June he became head of the *Ordnungspolizei*. In this capacity he was also in charge of *Ordnungspolizei* Head Office. On 20 April 1942 he was promoted to *SS-Oberstgruppenführer und Generaloberst der Polizei*. After the assassination of Heydrich, Daluege was named Deputy Reich Protector of Bohemia and Moravia, and as such was responsible for the massacre at Lidice. After the war Daluege was sentenced to death for crimes against the Czechoslovakian people and was hanged in Prague on 23 October 1946.

[6] As there were a number of localities where the religions were mixed, in recruiting it was not always possible to direct the Greek-Catholic men to the *Waffen-SS* and the Greek-Orthodox to the police. Thus, there was no religious affiliation within the division. The religious convictions of the Ukrainians led Himmler to authorize chaplains—unlike in most units of the SS. Over time nine Greek-Catholic chaplains served in the field with the *14. Waffen-Grenadier-Division der SS*.

[7] Not surprisingly, the wording of the entire text is extremely euphemistic. The "*recognition of their positive political attitude…*" was, as previously mentioned, nothing but nonsense. Plans to use Ukrainian officers and NCOs to build up the officer and NCO corps proved to be pure theory.

[8] Along with national movement reasons and the desire for a Ukrainian army, the original motivations behind the mass volunteering must have included the relatively good rations, but also fear of deportation to Germany. Even the UPA urged Ukrainians to join the division, as it had no means of training and equipping volunteers. It was hoped that the men would later return armed to the UPA. Of course, among the numerous students the idea of an autonomous Ukraine was the motivation for volunteering.

[9] On 21 June 1943 Berger informed Himmler that 26,436 volunteers had been mustered to date, but that just 3,281 of these were suitable for the division. That equated to about 12%. By 15 July 4,448 Ukrainians were taken in. Some of the men found unsuitable for service in the division found their way to the 4th – 7th Galician SS Volunteer Regiments of the Order Police, the guard complements of concentration camps or the labor service. The members of the division were not SS men in the true sense, as only a very few could meet the strict entrance requirements of the *Schutzstaffel*. SS suitability fell into one of three categories:

I Suitable for the order, German and Germanic persons fit for the SS, muster category: war service SS

II   Not suitable for the order, German and Germanic persons not fit for the SS, muster category: war service army.

III   Non-German, non-Germanic, no matter which muster category.

The members of the *SS-Division Galizien* were Ukrainians living in Galicia serving in the armed units of the SS. The division was therefore initially designated an SS Volunteer Division and later a Waffen-Division of the SS. On this topic, on 28 May 1944 Himmler wrote to the Chief of Security Police and SD in Berlin:

"In the Reich Security Head Office's criminal report of 26 May 1944 mention is made of a Ukrainian SS man in subparagraph 2. It should properly read: a Ukrainian serving in the armed units of the SS. I ask that the designation "SS man", which is so precious and revered to us, not be used in any report or in official and unofficial statements when referring to the many members of foreign nationality now organized under the SS."

[10] In recruiting, preference was given to volunteers who themselves or whose father had previously served in the Imperial Army. This was another example of the concept of continuing the tradition of the Austro-Hungarian Army. See also the *13. Waffen-Gebirgs-Division der SS Handschar (kroat* Nr. 1), whose members were supposed to carry on the tradition of the Bosnian regiments in the Imperial Army. See: Michaelis, Rolf: *Die Gebirgs-Divisionen der Waffen-SS*, Berlin 1998.

[11] The volunteers were liberally mustered. At a conference of political and military leaders—including *SS-Brigadeführer* Dr. Wächter, *Oberst* Bysanz, and *Generalleutnant der Polizei* Pfeffer-Wildenbruch—the following was stated:

"In view of the poor average quality of the local human material, especially from a Russian point of view, members of Racial Groups III and IV are also being admitted."

In the view of the Race and Settlement Head Office the racial groups were:

I	pure Nordic
II	primarily Nordic or Dalo-Nordic
III	Nordic or Dalo-Nordic with slight Alpine, Dinaric, or Mediterranean features
IV	mixed, primarily of Alpine origin
V	mixed, non-European origin

[12] SS-FHA, Org Diary No. 982/43 secret command matter of 30 July 1943.

[13] Dr. Wächter unsuccessfully opposed the designation Galicia, as it was a geographical term and not a racial one. Thus, Poles living in Galicia were also Galicians. He wanted to call the division Ukrainian, which Hitler and Himmler rejected, as it would have been in contradiction with existing policies in the east. In the political guidelines for the formation of the SS unit Dr. Wächter finally stated:

"Basically only volunteers of Ukrainian origin can be accepted. They should be living in the District of Galicia. It is not a precondition that they come from the District of Galicia or have lived there for a long time. It is sufficient if the responsible administrator or mayor confirms that the volunteer currently resides in the district administered by him.

Care is to be taken to ensure that the makeup of the new troops emphasizes the Ukrainian race, but—taking into consideration the of the area's constitutional status—the Ukrainians are not to be referred to in this context as allies, but it can be said that the soldiers of the SS Rifle Division Galicia are treated like German soldiers."

[14] In February 1945 the oath was amended to read:

"I swear to God this sacred oath, that in the struggle against bolshevism, to liberate my Ukrainian people, my Ukrainian homeland, I will render absolute obedience to the Supreme Commander of the Wehrmacht and all fighters of the young European races against bolshevism, and that as a brave soldier I will be ready to lay down my life for this oath at any time."

The oath specified action in the east. Nevertheless, elements of the Galician 4th – 7th SS Volunteer Regiments saw action in the west.

[15] Walter Schimana was born in Troppau on 12 March 1898. He fought in the First World War, first as a Reserve Officer Candidate. He joined the NSDAP in 1926, and from 1935 served with the police. Schimana was taken into the SS in 1939 (No. 337 753), and after the start of the war against Russia he became commander of the Security Police and SD in White Ruthenia. On 1 July 1942 he was promoted to *SS-Oberführer*, and on 9 November of the same year to *SS-Brigadeführer und Generalmajor der Polizei*. In March and April 1943 Schimana commanded an operational headquarters during the anti-partisan actions Lenz-South and Lenz-North. During his brief tenure as Commander of Order Police Paris he received the suffix *Generalmajor der Waffen-SS*. He was subsequently named head of the formation headquarters of the Galician SS Volunteer Division in Berlin. On 22 October 1943 Schimana took over the functions of Senior SS and Police Commander Greece, remaining in that position until 24 September of the following year. Promoted to *SS-Gruppenführer und Generalleutnant der Polizei* on 20 April 1944, from 5 October until the end of the war he served as Senior SS and Police Commander Danube. On 12 September 1948 he committed suicide in Salzburg prison while under investigation by the Allies.

[16] Collar patches and cap cockades with the trident were finally issued in 1945.

[17] SS-FHA, Dept. II, diary No. 1300/43.

[18] As the division headquarters was formed in Berlin and not moved to Debica until October 1943, there were numerous difficulties at the training camp.

[19] Bernhard Voß was born in Elberfeld on 29 June 1892. After training as a construction engineer, in 1914 he joined Magdeburg Pioneer Battalion 4. When the First World War ended he was discharged from the army with the rank of *Oberleutnant* and joined the police. Voß joined the NSDAP on 1 March 1933 and became a member of the SS on 2 April 1935. As head of the *SS-Junkerschule Tölz*, on 9 November 1935 he was promoted to *SS-Standartenführer*. After promotion to *SS-Oberführer* on 30 January 1938, he served in *SS-Oberabschnitt Ost* from 1 November 1938 until 15 August 1941. Until 1 November of the same year, Voß was a member of the *SS-Standortkommandantur Berlin* and from there commander of SS Training Camp Beneschau until 1 June 1942. Promoted to *SS-Brigadeführer* on 9 November 1942, on 5 September 1944 he was placed in charge of SS Training Camp Debica. In 1945 Voß was captured by the Americans. He was handed over to Czechoslovakia, where he was hanged in 1947.

[20] Fritz Freitag was born in Allenstein on 28 April 1894, the son of a railway official. After graduating from high school, he served in the First World War, attaining the rank of Reserve *Leutnant*. After a brief period with the *Freikorps*, on 3 February 1920 he joined the police force in Elbing. On 1 May 1933 he joined the NSDAP with party number 3,052,501. He was given general staff training, and from 8 May to 8 August 1941 served as 1st General Staff Officer in the Command Staff of the *Reichsführer-SS*. For the next 30 days he carried out the same duties for the 1st SS Motorized Infantry Brigade. He probably demonstrated himself to be unsuitable for the position of operations officer, for on 8 September 1941 he was sent to the SS-Division *Wiking* for familiarization with the position of regimental commander. At the end of the month he then took over SS Police Rifle Regiment 2 of the SS Police Division until 4 January 1943. On 5 January Freitag was placed in command of the SS Cavalry Division. A dispute arose with Himmler, who disagreed with Freitag's style of command and threatened to relieve him of command of the division.

From 21 April to 18 August 1943 followed employment as commander of the 2nd SS Infantry Brigade. From the next day on Freitag, with the rank of *SS-Oberführer*, was placed in command of the SS Police Division, and on 21 October 1943 he was made commander of the 14th Galician SS Volunteer Infantry Division. On 29 January 1944 the SS-FHA issued orders for *SS-Oberführer* Freitag to attend the 9th Division Commander Course in Hirschberg. On 20 April of the same year Freitag was promoted to *SS-Brigadeführer und Generalmajor der Waffen-SS*. Six months later he was named commander of the *14. Waffen-Grenadier-Division der SS*—a post for which he had little enthusiasm. After receiving the German Cross in Gold on 30 April 1943, on 30 September he was awarded the Knight's Cross with Oak Leaves. *SS-Brigadeführer* Freitag spent the night of 8-9 May 1945 in an inn and was seen leaving by the innkeeper. One month later he was found by a woman tending cattle—he had shot himself.

[21] Effective 30 January 1944, the Ukrainian 204th Police Battalion, which had previously served as a guard battalion at the Heidelager training camp, was attached to the *14. Galizische SS-Freiwilligen-Infanterie-Division*.

[22] Wilhelm Koppe was born in Hildesheim on 15 June 1896, and after the war ran a grocery store. He joined the NSDAP in 1930 with the number 305,584, and in 1931 the SA. One year later he received membership number 29,955 in the SS, and on 23 August 1934 achieved the rank of *SS-Brigadeführer*. Promoted to *SS-Gruppenführer* on 13 September 1936, from 26 October 1939 Koppe was Senior SS and Police Commander Warthe. In winter 1941 he arrived at the Chelmno extermination camp, and on 30 January 1942 was promoted to *SS-Obergruppenführer und General der Polizei*. From 9 November 1943 he performed the duties of Senior SS and Police Commander East. On 1 July 1944, while in this post, Koppe received the rank suffix "*General der Waffen-SS.*" After a brief period as Senior SS and Police Commander South in April 1945, at the end of the war he went underground with a false name. In 1961 he was recognized and arrested. His case was dismissed for lack of evidence in 1966. Koppe died on 2 July 1975.

[23] The 6th Galician SS Volunteer Regiment was established on 6 August 1943 from the second intake of volunteers from the Lvov District. Personnel from the disbanded 32nd Police Rifle Regiment formed the core of the regiment. The headquarters and II Battalion were based at Gumbinnen, the I Battalion in Sudauen, and the III Battalion in Grajewo. In November 1943 the units were briefly transferred to Headquarters, 1st Army in France. At the end of January 1944 the regiment received orders to move to Heidelager training camp.

The 7th Galician SS Volunteer Regiment was established by the Commander of the Order Police Paris on 29 September 1943 using Ukrainian volunteers sent there. Regimental headquarters, along with the I and III Battalions, occupied quarters in Salies de Béarn, near Bayonne, the II Battalion in Orthez. The regiment was also transferred to Heidelager on 31 January 1944.

[24] Walter Model was born in Genthin on 24 January 1891. He began his military career on 27 February 1909 as an officer candidate, and one year later he was named a *Leutnant* in the 58th Infantry Regiment. He served in the First World War, and afterwards in the *Reichswehr*. Promoted to *Generalmajor* on 1 March 1938, Model was named chief-of-staff of the IV Army Corps on 10 November of the same year. On 1 April 1940, while serving as chief-of-staff of the 16th Army, he was promoted to *Generalleutnant*. On 13 November he was given command of the 3rd Panzer Division, and on 1 October 1941 he was promoted to *General der Panzertruppen* and made commander of XXXXI Panzer Corps. Model was promoted to *Generaloberst* on 16 January 1942 and placed in command of the 9th Army. Named commander-in-chief of Army Group North on 9 January 1944, on 1 March of the same year he was promoted to *Generalfeldmarschall*. At the end of the month he was placed in command of Army Group North Ukraine. Finally, from 28 June 1944 he was commander-in-chief of Army Groups B and West. Decorated with the Knight's Cross with Oak Leaves, Swords and Diamonds, in 1945 Model chose to commit suicide in the Ruhr Pocket.

[25] The corps was commanded by *General der Infanterie* Arthur Hauffe. Born in Wittgendorf, near Lvov, on 20 December 1891, he joined the military as an officer candidate in summer 1912. With the rank of *Oberst*, from 26 September 1939 to 5 February 1940 he was chief-of-staff of the XXV Army Corps. He later held the same post in the XXXVIII Panzer Corps. After a period as chief-of-staff (*Generalmajor*) of the Military Mission in Rumania he was promoted to *Generalleutnant* (1 January 1943), and from 7 February to 20 August 1943 commanded the 46th Infantry Division. While in that position Hauffe was awarded the Knight's Cross of the Iron Cross on 25 July. On 7 September 1943 he became commanding general of XIII Army Corps, and on 1 November of the same year was promoted to *General der Infanterie*. Hauffe was killed on 22 July 1944 during an attempted breakout from the Brody Pocket.

[26] This included members of the population able to work.

[27] Gerhard Lindemann was born in Verden on 2 August 1896. In August 1914 he joined the 7th Field Artillery Regiment as a volunteer, and one year later was promoted to *Leutnant* in the 158th Infantry Regiment. He was released from active service on 31 March 1920. Lindemann rejoined the *Wehrmacht* as a *Hauptmann* on 1 July 1934. When the Second World War began he was a battalion commander in the 269th Infantry Division. From 1 January 1941 he held the same post in the 102nd Infantry Division, and on 1 August of that year he was promoted to *Oberstleutnant*. Placed in command of the 216th Infantry Regiment at the end of December, on 1 April 1942 he was promoted to *Oberst*. In November/December 1943 he attended a division commander course, and in April 1944 was placed in command of *Korpsabteilung C*. From the end of May to 22 July 1944 he commanded the 361st Infantry Division. Decorated with the Knight's Cross with Oak Leaves, Lindemann was released from Soviet captivity on 7 October 1955 and returned to Germany.

[28] Otto Lasch was born in Pless on 25 June 1893. Several weeks after the start of "Operation Barbarossa," Lasch, then an *Oberst* and commander of the 43rd Infantry Regiment, was awarded the Knight's Cross. Promotion to *Generalmajor* followed on 1 August 1942, and on 27 September of that year he was named commander of the 217th Infantry Division. Promoted to *Generalleutnant* on 1 April 1943, on 20 November he took over the 349th Infantry Division. Lasch was named commanding general of LXIV Army Corps on 1 September 1944, and two months later he assumed command of I Army Corps, and later Fortress Königsberg. On 9 April 1945 he surrendered the fortress, and in his absence Hitler demoted him and sentenced him to death for cowardice in the face of the enemy. His family was held responsible for his political crimes. Lasch returned from Soviet captivity at the end of October 1955.

[29] Heino Baron von Künsberg was awarded the Knight's Cross on 16 September 1943 while commanding the 188th Infantry Regiment with the rank of *Oberstleutnant*.

[30] Because of the poor relations between Freitag and the Ukrainians in his division, neither the Ukrainian Military Board nor the Ukrainian Senior Military Board congratulated him on receiving the Knight's Cross! That speaks for itself. In his division order of 19 October 1944 Freitag wrote:

"*Men of my division!*

The Führer has awarded me the Knight's Cross of the Iron Cross.

I wear this high decoration for all the brave and exemplary German and Ukrainian officers, NCOs and men of the division, who upheld the soldierly virtues through their commitment, attitude and character in those difficult days at Brody, and thus established the tradition for the 1st Ukrainian Division.

To the Germans in my division my decoration represents the highest praise and recognition for the work you have done in building this unit and your bravery ion the struggle for the existence of our people.

For the Ukrainians it constitutes equal recognition and certainty that the Führer recognizes all the brave acts by the Ukrainians and even more, that he gives the fullest recognition to actions of the Ukrainians in battle for their people and homeland, which is to be made free again.

We all wish to renew our promise to the Führer, to continue our joint struggle until victory is achieved over the bolshevist hordes and their Jewish-plutocrat helpers."

The wording *highest praise* for the German core personnel, but only *equal recognition* for the Ukrainian soldiers clearly illustrates Freitag's relative opinion.

[31] Of this, former *SS-Obersturmführer* Dornbusch recalled:

"*Freitag was perhaps a good senior police officer and official, but no dynamic division commander. His aversion to leading a foreign division probably had its basis in his origins. He was born an East Prussian (border land), and these people were very conscious of nationality and homeland and mistrustful of the border inhabitants on the other side, which he apparently carried over to the Ukrainians. Freitag may also have been a weak man with a little strength of nerve, like several other officers in the division (my company commander SS-Obersturmführer Schneller or my battalion commander SS-Sturmbannführer Kleinow, who ordered his driver get his car ready whenever there was the slightest sign of unrest at the front).*"

[32] Most of these deserters made contact with the UPA and continued their resistance in its ranks. There was certainly nothing like "*internally anchored cowardice.*"

[33] There are contradictions in Himmler's statements. The division accomplished all the tasks given it, despite soldiers who were *"psychologically weak and inconstant, to whom the manly and military German virtues are foreign."*

[34] Hans Jüttner was born in Schmiegel on 2 March 1894. After studying banking, in 1914 he voluntarily joined West Prussian Fusilier Regiment No. 37. After serving in Reserve Infantry Regiment No. 267 and the replacement battalion of the 153rd Infantry Regiment, he was placed in charge of an instructional detachment in Turkey. Finally he was sent to Syria, Mesopotamia, and Iraq. After serving in the *Grenzschutz Ost*, in January 1920 Jüttner was released from military service. He was active in commerce until 1929, and on 1 February 1931 joined the SA. Jüttner remained in the SA until 15 April 1934, serving as the organization's head of training. He was taken into the SS with the rank of *SS-Hauptsturmführer* and served in the headquarters of *I./SS-Standarte Deutschland*. Promoted several times, on 30 January 1943 Jüttner was named head of the SS-FHA with the rank of *SS-Gruppenführer*. He was promoted to *SS-Obergruppenführer und General der Waffen-SS* on 21 June 1943. After 20 July 1944 he was permanent deputy of the *Reichsführer-SS*, and on 30 October of that year was awarded the Knight's Cross of the War Merit Cross. He died in Bad Tölz on 24 May 1965.

[35] Field command post, diary No. III/1294/44 of 7 August 1944.

[36] SS-FHA, diary No. 2880 secret command matter of 5 September 1944.

[37] SS-FHA, diary No. II/8602/44.

[38] The Galician 4th SS Volunteer Regiment was established in July 1943. The headquarters and I Battalion were stationed in Zabern, II Battalion in Saaralben, and III Battalion in Fischweiler, near Trier. III Battalion was deployed to the Netherlands in February 1944. By an order issued on 9 June 1944 the unit's enlisted men were taken into the *Waffen-Ausbildungs- und Ersatz-Regiment der SS*.

The Galician 5th Volunteer Regiment was also established in July 1943. I Battalion was formed by I Battalion/32nd Police Rifle Regiment. The units were employed against partisans near Lublin-Hrubieszow and Cholm, and by an order issued on 9 June 1944 were transferred to the *Waffen-Ausbildungs- und Ersatz-Regiment der SS*.

[39] Numerically there were sufficient new recruits from the evacuated areas as well as foreign workers; however, the young Ukrainians lacked the motivation of their comrades in 1943. Many of them had no interest in serving in the German armed services or the *Waffen-SS*.

[40] The German military marched into Czechoslovakia on 13 March 1939, and the following day Hitler proclaimed the Protectorate of Bohemia and Moravia. In the eastern part of the former Czechoslovakian Republic, Slovakia was an autonomous state. While German and Czech police pursued enemies of the regime in the Protectorate, in Slovakia it was much easier to form a resistance movement. Despite this, the underground groups only became active after the invasion of the Soviet Union on 22 June 1941. In the period that followed, the groups' ranks were swollen by workers, escaped Soviet, Polish, and French POWs and, as the war went on, deserters from the Slovakian military. In 1944 the decision was made to bring down the Hitler-friendly Hlinka regime with Soviet help. The Red Army neared the Slovakian border in August, and at the end of the month nationalists stepped into the open in many towns. Restoration of the situation through the entry of German troops into Slovakia—as in Hungary—was not possible because of a shortage of forces. Nevertheless, plans were made to disarm the Slovakian Army under the code name Potato Harvest.

When the situation deteriorated further, German units, including elements of the 178th Panzer Division (Battle Group von Ohlen), moved into the country. State President Tiso justified this as necessary help from Germany in suppressing a communist uprising in Slovakia.

On 31 August 1944 Army Group North Ukraine, which was in command of eastern Slovakia, ordered two more battle groups into the country, which caused the uprising to falter. The previous day the commander-in-chief of Army Group North Ukraine had ordered the ruthless suppression of the uprising.

Although the German commander in Slovakia was aware of the subversive activities in the country, the open outbreak of the national uprising took him by surprise; consequently, his initial actions were no more than interim measures. On 2 September 1944 *SS-Obergruppenführer* Gottlob Berger, head of the SS Head Office in Berlin, who was on his way back from Croatia, assumed command in West Slovakia and held the naïve opinion that the revolt could be put down in four days.

The Red Army supported the partisans with Slovakian exile troops delivered by aircraft, as well as an attack on 8 September at the Dukla Pass, in the northeast of Slovakia. Although the Soviet troops initially achieved little and did not enter Slovakia until October 1944, the offensive at least had a positive effect on the morale of the rebels.

On 14 September *SS-Obergruppenführer* Höfle relieved Berger, who as an administrator had failed to end the uprising. On 20 September all German troops in Slovakia came under the command of the German commander in Slovakia (Höfle).

The Red Army's advance over the Carpathians and through Hungary, where they approached Debrecen in mid-October 1944, led Höfle to request additional troops. The German commander in Slovakia ultimately commanded about 50,000 men, which went on the offensive in mid-October 1944.

[41] SS-FHA diary No. 3411/44 secret command matter.

[42] Hermann Höfle was born on 12 September 1898. On 1 August 1933 he joined the NSDAP and its SS. On 1 October 1944, then holding the rank of *SS-Obergruppenführer und General der Waffen-SS*, he took over the post of Senior SS and Police Commander Slovakia from Berger. He was hanged in Slovakia in 1947.

[43] Friedrich-Wilhelm von Loeper was born in Prieborn on 3 August 1888. He began his military career on 22 March 1906 as a *Leutnant* in the 1st Grenadier Regiment. Promoted to *Oberst* on 1 April 1934, on 1 October 1935 he was named commander of the 64th Infantry Regiment. In the Polish Campaign he led the 1st Light Division with the rank of *Generalmajor* (1 August 1938), and on 25 October 1939 took command of the 81st Infantry Division. Following promotion to *Generalleutnant* on 1 September 1940, from 5 October 1940 until 15 April 1942 he commanded the 10th Infantry Division, receiving the Knight's Cross with Oak Leaves on 29 September 1941. On 1 May 1943 he was named commander of the 178th Reserve Panzer Division, and from August 1944 led the Tatra Division. His last command was the Ludwig Division from January 1945.

[44] For a history of this unit see: Michaelis, Rolf: *Das SS-Sonderkommando Dirlewanger*, Berlin 1999.[2]

[45] The Soviet offensive against Budapest began on 5 December 1944. Southwest of the city the 4th Guards Army attacked the 6th Army, and north of the city in the area of the 8th Army, in command there, Army Group Plijew. On 31 December 1944 the latter consisted of:

XXIX Army Corps with the 15th and 76 Infantry Divisions and the 8th *Jäger* (light infantry) Division,

Feldherrnhalle Panzer Corps with the SS-Brigade Dirlewanger, 46th Infantry Division, 4th and 18th SS Divisions and the 24th Panzer Division,

IX Hungarian Army Corps with the 9th Light Border Infantry Division and the Hungarian 27th Division.

[46] This was established at the Böhmen training camp beginning in July 1944.

[47] The first defensive battle lasted from 10 to 30 August 1944. At times the IV SS Panzer Corps faced three Soviet armies whose aim was to force a breakthrough to Warsaw. The second defensive battle lasted from 31 August to 22 September 1944.

[48] Karl Ullrich was born in Saargemünd on 1 December 1910, and from 1929 to 1933 he studied mechanical engineering. He joined the SA in 1931, and one year later the SS. On 1 June 1933 he joined the 19th Infantry Regiment as a volunteer, and six months later committed himself to service in the armed SS (*SS-Verfügungstruppe*). On 1 April 1936 he achieved the rank of *SS-Untersturmführer*. *SS-Hauptsturmführer* Ullrich took part in the fighting in Poland with the SS Pioneer Battalion, and in May 1941 he became commander of the 3rd SS Pioneer Battalion. Awarded the Knight's Cross on 19 February 1942, on 10 November 1943 *SS-Obersturmbannführer* Ullrich assumed command of the 6th SS Panzer-

Grenadier Regiment 6 *Theodor Eicke*. In that post he received the Knight's Cross with Oak Leaves on 14 May 1944. Promoted to *SS-Standartenführer* on 29 July 1944, from 9 October he commanded the 5. *SS-Panzer-Division* Wiking, and on 20 April 1945 was promoted to *SS-Oberführer*. Ullrich died in Bad Reichenhall on 8 May 1996.

[49] SS-FHA, diary No. 550/45 secret command matter of 26 January 1945.

[50] There were three march groups. The first, which was under the command of *SS-Brigadeführer* Freitag, consisted of:

- *Waffen-Grenadier-Regiment der SS 29* and *30*
- *Waffen-Grenadier-Ausbildungs-und Ersatz-Regiment der SS 14*
- *Waffen-Artillerie-Regiment der SS 14*
- 14th SS Signals Battalion
- elements of the 14th SS Anti-Tank Battalion
- division supply units

March Group B was under the command of *SS-Standartenführer* Pannier and consisted of:

- Waffen-Grenadier-Regiment der SS 31
- 14th SS Fusilier Battalion
- 14th SS Pioneer Battalion
- 14th SS Field Replacement Battalion

March Group C under *SS-Sturmbannführer* Kaschner consisted of the division's vehicles and was transported by rail.

[51] Erwin Rösener was born in Schwerte on 2 February 1902. He joined the Nazi Party in 1926 (No. 46,771) and the SA in 1929. He soon moved to the SS (membership number 3,575), and on 9 November 1939 achieved the rank of *SS-Brigadeführer*. From 16 December 1940 until 15 December 1941 Rösener was Senior SS and Police Commander Rhine. On 15 April 1941 the suffix "*Generalmajor der Polizei*" was added to his title. Promoted to *SS-Gruppenführer und Generalleutnant der Polizei* on 9 November 1941, on 16 December of that year he became Senior SS and Police Commander *Alpenland*. While in that post he was promoted to *SS-Obergruppenführer und General der Polizei und Waffen-SS* on 1 August 1944. Rösener was hanged in Yugoslavia on 31 August 1946.

[52] With little equipment and poor rations, the rebels also had little will to fight.

[53] The Soviet forces had advanced far to the west on both sides of Lake Balaton and were able to march into the Feldbach area (east of Graz).

[54] OKH, Operations Department I a, No. 450224/45 secret command matter/C.O. of 23 March 1945.

[55] Johannes Göhler was born in Bischofswerda on 15 September 1918. On 17 September 1943 he was awarded the Knight's Cross while serving as an *SS-Obersturmführer* and commander of 4./*SS-Reiter-Regiment 15*. Promoted to *SS-Hauptsturmführer* 9 November 1943, in August 1944 he became adjutant to the Führer's *Waffen-SS* liaison officer, *SS-Gruppenführer* Fegelein. Göhler was promoted to *SS-Sturmbannführer* on 21 December 1944.

[56] Wilhelm Burgdorf was born in Fürstenwalde on 15 February 1895. He joined the 12th Grenadier Regiment as an officer candidate on 1 August 1914, and on 18 April was promoted to *Leutnant*. After serving in the *Reichswehr*, on 1 October 1937 he became adjutant in the IX Army Corps. After promotion to *Oberstleutnant* on 1 August 1938, in summer 1940 he took over the 529th Infantry Regiment. In that post he was promoted to *Oberst* on 1 September 1940 and received the Knight's Cross on 29 September 1941. He became a department head in the Army Personnel Office on 1 May 1942, and on 1 October 1942 he was promoted to *Generalmajor* and made deputy head of the APO. Promoted to *Generalleutnant* on 1 October 1943, on 1 October 1944 he took over the Army Personnel Office. One month later he achieved the rank of *General der Infanterie*. Burgdorf shot himself in Berlin on 2 May 1945.

[57] He meant the 20th SS Waffen-Grenadier Division (Estonian No. 1), which had been destroyed in Silesia.

[58] Heinrich Borgmann was born in 1912. He was awarded the Knight's Cross as an *Oberleutnant* and commander of the 9./Inf.Rgt. 46 on 19 July 1940 and the Oak Leaves as a *Hauptmann* and commander of III./Inf.Rgt. 46 on 11 February 1942. On 26 September 1943 *Major* Borgmann was assigned to the *Wehrmacht Adjutantur* and one month later became the Führer's army adjutant. He was promoted to *Oberstleutnant* on 1 January 1944, and in March was placed in command of a *Volks-Grenadier-Division* in the west. In April 1945, General Staff *Oberst* Borgmann was killed in a strafing attack.

[59] Göhler erred here, for the enlisted men *30. Waffen-Grenadier-Division der SS (russ. Nr. 2)* were (White) Russian and had nothing to do with the Galician/Ukrainian division.

[60] Ulrich de Maiziére was born in 1912. Promoted to *Oberstleutnant* in July 1943, in November 1944 he was operations officer of an army in the west. On 15 February 1945 he was transferred to the Army General Staff/Ia Operations Section, and in May 1945 to the *Wehrmacht* Operations Staff. He joined the newly-created *Bundeswehr* in 1955.

[61] A comparison with the authorized equipment of an infantry division according to the 1944 table of organization shows that, at least in terms of armament, the division was almost fully equipped—an unusual condition at that time.

(a) Personnel Strength

division command	186 men	division map section	8 men
military police squad	33 men	grenadier regiments	5,961 men
fusilier battalion	708 men	anti-tank battalion	484 men
artillery regiment	2,013 men	pioneer battalion	620 men
signals battalion	379 men	field replacement btn.	925 men
supply units	1,415 men	**Total:**	**12,772 men**

(b) Armament

rifles	8,598	K 43 self-loading rifles	309
sniper rifles	513	anti-tank rocket launchers	108
pistols	2,013	submachine-guns	1,595
light machine-guns	614	heavy machine-guns	102
light mortars 81.4 mm	54	heavy mortars 120 mm	32
20 mm light anti-aircraft guns	13	flamethrowers	22
50 mm anti-tank guns	1	75 mm anti-tank guns	22
75 mm light infantry guns 19	150	mm heavy infantry guns	6
105 mm light howitzers	34	150 mm heavy howitzers	9
flare pistols	389	rifle grenade launchers	489

(c) Vehicles

motorcycles	118	motorcycles with sidecar	36
Kettenkrafträder	14	4WD cars	136
cars	31	busses	9
4WD trucks	149	trucks	221
assault guns	10	*Raupenschlepper Ost*	58
prime movers	3	*Maultier* trucks	10
trailers	40	horse-drawn vehicles	1,365
other vehicles	501	bicycles	678

(d) Horses

riding horses	802	light draught horses	2,537
heavy draught horses	523	very heavy draught horses	117

[62] This was established in the Krems – Melk area in March 1945 using personnel released by the 1st and 4th Parachute Divisions, personnel from the *Luftwaffe* officer schools in Berlin-Gatow, Straubing, Fürstenfeldbruck, Dresden, and Ergolding, plus personnel from the

flying units and ground organization of Air Fleet 6. As of 26 March 1945, however, the 10th Parachute Division had only about 1,000 soldiers.

[63] Gustav Harteneck was born in Landau on 27 July 1892. On 7 August 1914 he joined the Bavarian Army as an officer candidate, and on 25 August 1915 became a *Leutnant* in the 5th Chevalier Regiment. He served in the *Reichswehr* after the First World War, and on 1 March 1937 was promoted to *Oberstleutnant*. On 10 November of the following year he was commander of the 9th Cavalry Regiment, and as such he was promoted to the rank of *Oberst* on 1 August 1939. At the start of the Second World War he was 1st General Staff Officer of the 1st Army, and on 10 November 1940 was appointed chief-of-staff of the XXVII Army Corps. On 26 October 1941 he became chief-of-staff of the 2nd Army, and on 1 February 1942 Hitler promoted him to *Generalmajor*. Named *Generalleutnant* on 1 April 1944, on 10 June he took command of the Cavalry Corps. Awarded the Knight's Cross, on 1 September 1944 Harteneck was named *General der Kavallerie*.

[64] Josef von Radowitz was born in Frankfurt/Main on 29 July 1899. He joined the military as an officer candidate in 1917, and from 6 September 1918 served as a *Leutnant* in the 20th Dragoon Regiment. The following year he was demobilized. On 1 April 1924 von Radowitz was reactivated as a *Leutnant* in the 18th Cavalry Regiment. He was promoted to *Oberstleutnant* on March 1941, and from 1 February 1942 to 1 April 1943 he served in the staff of the 2nd Panzer Army. Promoted to *Oberst* on 1 March 1942, he commanded the 28th Panzer-Grenadier Regiment until 1 April 1944. In June 1944 he became commander of the 23rd Panzer Division, and on 1 September was promoted to *Generalmajor*. On 17 September he was awarded the Knight's Cross of the Iron Cross. His promotion to *Generalleutnant* was announced with an effective date of 1 March 1945. On the day of the surrender he was awarded the Knight's Cross with Oak Leaves. In 1955 he joined the *Bundeswehr* and served as head of recruiting. He died in Bad Wiesee in 1956.

[65] Radkersburg first came under Soviet artillery fire on 4 April 1945. The battle for the town began eight days later. After blowing the Mur bridge, during the night of 14-15 April the soldiers evacuated the town and pulled back toward Oberradkersburg.

[66] *Waffen-Grenadier-Ausbildungs-und Ersatz-Regiment der SS 14* had meanwhile moved into the area around Völkermarkt.

[67] Herrmann Balck was born in Danzig on 7 December 1893. He was named *Generalmajor* on 1 August 1942, at which time he commanded the 11th Panzer Division. Promoted to *Generalleutnant* on 1 January 1943, in April he was appointed commander of the *Großdeutschland Division* for three months. Balck was promoted to *General der Panzertruppen* on1 November 1943, after which he took over the XXXX Panzer Corps for a brief period. He commanded the XXXXVIII Panzer Corps until August 1944, when he became commander-in-chief of the 4th Panzer Army. In September 1944 he commanded Army Group C for a few days, and then the 6th Army, which together with the 2nd Hungarian Army was sometimes called Army Group Balck until the end of the war. Balck had received the Knight's Cross on 3 June 1940. The Oak Leaves followed on 22 December 1942, the Swords on 4 March 1943, and the Diamonds on 31 August 1944. He died on 29 November 1982.

[68] Herbert Gille was born in Gandersheim on 8 March 1897. At the age of 14 he joined the Royal Prussian Cadet Corps. In 1915 he became a *Leutnant* in the 2nd Baden Field Artillery Regiment No. 30. Still holding that rank, he was discharged from military service in 1919. In December 1931 he joined the SS, and on 20 April 1933 attained the rank of *SS-Untersturmführer*. After holding various positions in the *SS-Verfügungstruppe* (armed SS), on 15 November 1940 *SS-Obersturmbannführer* Gille took over the SS Artillery Regiment *Wiking*. After promotion to *SS-Standartenführer* (30 January 1941), *SS-Oberführer* (1 October 1941), and *SS-Brigadeführer und Generalmajor der Waffen-SS* (9 November 1942), Gille was placed in command of the *SS-Panzergrenadier-Division Wiking* on 1 May 1943. In that post he was promoted to *SS-Gruppenführer und Generalleutnant der Waffen-SS*. From 6 August 1944 he commanded the IV SS Panzer Corps, and on 9 November of that year he was promoted to *SS-Obergruppenführer und General der*

Waffen-SS. He received the Knight's Cross of the Iron Cross on 8 October 1942 and the Oak Leaves on 1 November 1943. The Swords followed on 20 February 1944 and the Diamonds on 19 April 1944. Gille was captured by the Americans near Radstadt and was released on 21 May 1948. He died in Stemmen on 26 December 1966.

[69] Also see Appendix 4.

[70] The Ukrainians living there were supposed to be gradually made more Polish. Polish became the official language and the Ukrainian Church was banned. On 20 April 1940 the General Governor reopened the old cathedral in Cholm, a symbol of the Ukrainian Church taken away by the Poles, much to the joy of the Ukrainian population.

[71] These partisans formed the basis of the later Ukrainian Rebel Army (UPA).

[72] Stephan Bandera was born near Kalush on 1 January 1909. He was chairman of the OUN, which initially opposed the Polish occupation of the West Ukraine, later the Soviet, and at times also the German occupying power. After 1945 Bandera lived in Munich under the name Popel and from there reorganized the OUN. On 15 October 1959 Bogdan Stashinski, an agent of the KGB, killed the émigré leader in Munich with a poison bullet fired from a pistol.

[73] Prof. Dr. Lev Rebet was born on 3 March 1912. After the war he became the chief editor of the Ukrainian exile newspapers "Ukrainski Samostinik" and "Sucasna Ukraina" in Munich. He was murdered there by Soviet KGB agent Stashinski on 12 October 1957.

[74] Dr. Hans Frank was born on 23 May 1900. In 1919 he was a student at the University of Munich and was already a member of Hitler's inner circle. He later led the National-Socialist Lawyers Association (sic!) and was head of the NSDAP Legal Office. In the *Allgemeine-SS* he achieved the rank of *SS-Gruppenführer*, and as General Governor of Poland he attended numerous meetings concerning the campaign against the Jews and the final solution. After the war he was hanged in Poland.

[75] The General Government was created by Hitler's order on 12 October 1939 and consisted of five districts: Cracow, Warsaw, Lublin, Radom, and Galicia. Nearly 18 million people lived in the five districts, which encompassed an area of 150,000 km^2. (That was equivalent to the population of the former East Germany.)

[76] Erich Koch was born in Elberfeld on 19 June 1896. After taking part in the First World War he was a member of a *Freikorps* in Upper Silesia. He joined the Nazi Party in 1922, and by 1928 was a member of the Ruhr District Command. On 1 October 1928 he was named District Leader of East Prussia. In 1930 he became a deputy in the Reichstag and Prussian councilor of state, and in 1933 he was named Senior President of East Prussia. In November 1941 Koch became Reich Commissar for the Ukraine. After the war he disappeared under a false name, but he was uncovered in Hamburg in 1949. Koch was handed over to Poland in 1950 and sentenced to death nine years later. The sentence was ultimately commuted to life in prison, and in 1986 he died in his nineties.

[77] The Ukrainians, who had greeted the German forces as liberators from Stalinist oppression, were soon forced to realize that they were now being exploited and suppressed by them. This led to the foundation of the Ukrainian Rebel Army, or UPA, in October 1942. It succeeded in gaining control of large areas away from the major transportation centers. Stalin also sent communist partisans into the country with the task of intimidating the civilian population. The efforts of the UPA, which ultimately numbered about 200,000 fighters, were directed mainly against the communist partisans, as they were seen as the more dangerous opponent.

[78] Andrei Vlasov was born in Lomakino (Novgorod District) on 1 September 1900, the son of a farmer. After attending a seminary, in 1919 he joined the Red Army. Ten years later he was a battalion commander, and in 1930 he joined the Communist Party. In 1938-1940 he served as a military advisor with the rank of colonel. Promoted to Major-General in June 1940, in November 1941 he took over the 20th Army, which successfully defended Moscow. Promoted to Lieutenant-General in January 1942, in July he was captured at the Volkhov River as commander of the 2nd Shock Army. Until the end of the war he tried to convince the Germans of the importance of Russian help in the struggle against Stalin. Hitler was extremely skeptical of this and made only minor concessions. The so-called Prague Manifesto of November 1944 was essentially a propaganda tool and had no effect.

The German leader's skepticism proved well-founded, for in May 1945 the 1ˢᵗ Division of the Russian Liberation Army (ROA) turned against the German troops in Prague. Captured by the Soviets, Vlasov was hanged in August 1946.

[79] At a meeting between Vlasov and Shandruk they agreed that Shandruk should be responsible for West-Ukrainian Galicia and Vlasov for the East Ukraine.

[80] *Waffen-SS* Gazette of 15 January 1945.

[81] On 28 March 1945 General Shandruk visited the 2ⁿᵈ Division. It was in the process of being formed, and at that time had one regiment of about 1,900 soldiers. It recruited mainly from released Ukrainian POWs and foreign workers, and was located in Nimegk, near Berlin. First elements of the formation, ultimately renamed the Ukrainian Tank-Destroyer Brigade, were committed in Czechoslovakia in the northern part of Army Group Schörner.

[82] Rudolf Pannier was born in Gera on 10 July 1897. He joined the military as a volunteer on 1 May 1917 and fought in France and Russia. After the First World War he was a member of various *Freikorps*, and in February 1920 he moved to the Hamburg Police Department. On 15 December 1933 he left active police service as a *Hauptmann der Schutzpolizei* and worked as a bank salesman. Pannier was reactivated on 6 June 1940, and until 1941 was air defense officer in Posen. Assigned to the SS Police Division in Russia, he was awarded the Iron Cross, 1ˢᵗ Class in December 1941 and led the I Battalion of SS Police Rifle Regiment 2. Involved in the fierce fighting at the Volkhov River, on 11 May 1942 he was awarded the Knight's Cross of the Iron Cross with the rank of *SS-Sturmbannführer und Major der Schutzpolizei*. In June-July 1942 Pannier worked as chief-of-staff to the commander of the *Waffen-SS* in the Netherlands, and in 1943 became commander of the recruiting depot and formation staff of the SS Police Division at the Debica training camp. As head of Supply Post Russia-Center, on 28 April 1944 he was awarded the German Cross in Gold. Assigned to the formation of Estonian and Latvian units at the beginning of 1944, in September of that year he took over *Waffen-Grenadier-Regiment der SS 31* at the Neuhammer training camp. Severely wounded near Straden, he was captured by the Soviets in the military hospital in Wagna, near Leibnitz. From there he was handed over to the western allies. Pannier died in Hamburg on 19 August 1978.

[84] After June 1944 the prefix "Waffen" was added to the rank designations of foreign soldiers serving in armed units of the S instead of the designation "SS" or "Volunteer."

Bibliography

Anders, Karl: Mord auf Befehl, Tübingen 1963

Birm, Ruth: Die Höheren SS- und Polizeiführer, Tübingen 1985

Dallin, Alexander: Deutsche Herrschaft in Rußland, Düsseldorf 1958

Doroschenko, Dmytro: Die Ukraine und Deutschland, München 1994

Friessner, Hans: Verratene Schlachten, Hamburg 1956

Grasmug, Rudolf, u.a.: So war es, Feldbach 1996

Haupt, Wemer: Die Heeresgruppe Mitte, Dorheim 1968

Heiber, Helmut (Hrsg.): Lagebesprechungen im Führerhauptquartier, Milnchen 1964

Heike, Wolf-Dietrich: Sie wollten die Freiheit, Dorheim o.J.

Hunczak, Taras: The Ukrainian Division Galicia, Chatham o.J.

Klietmann, Dr. K.-G.: Die Waffen-SS, Osnabrück 1965

Krätschmer, Ernst-Günther: Die Ritterkreuzträger der Waffen-SS, Pr. Oldendorf 1982

Michaelis, Rolf: Die Gebirgs-Divisionen der Waffen-SS, Berlin 1998[2]

Michaelis, Rolf: Die Grenadier-Divisionen der Waffen-SS (I-III), Erlangen 1994/95

Michaelis, Rolf: Das SS-Sonderkommando Dirlewanger, Berlin 1999[2]

Neulen, Hans Wemer: An deutscher Seite, München 1985

Preradovich, Nikolaus von: Die Generale der Waffen-SS, Berg 1985

Ukrainischer Verlag (Hrsg.): Russischer Kolonialismus in der Ukraine, Munchen 1962

Register of Names